D1552418

Changing

Selected Writings 8

RICHARD BERENGARTEN was born in London in 1943, into a family of musicians. He has lived in Italy, Greece, the USA and former Yugoslavia. His perspectives as a poet combine English, French, Mediterranean, Jewish, Slavic, American and Oriental influences.

Under the name RICHARD BURNS, he has published more than 25 books. In the 1970s, he founded and ran the international Cambridge Poetry Festival. In the UK he has received the Eric Gregory Award, the Wingate-Jewish Quarterly Award for Poetry, the Keats Poetry Prize, and the Yeats Club Prize. In Serbia, he has received the international Morava Charter Poetry Prize and the Great Lesson Award, and in Macedonia, the Manada Prize. He has been Writer-in-Residence at the international Eliot-Dante Colloquium in Florence, Arts Council Writer-in-Residence at the Victoria Centre in Gravesend, Royal Literary Fund Fellow at Newnham College, Cambridge, and a Royal Literary Fund Project Fellow. He has been Visiting Associate Professor at the University of Notre Dame and British Council Lecturer in Belgrade, first at the Centre for Foreign Languages and then at the Philological Faculty. He is a Fellow of the English Association, a Bye-Fellow at Downing College, Cambridge, and an Academic Associate at Pembroke College, Cambridge. His poems have been translated into more than 90 languages.

ALSO BY RICHARD BERENGARTEN

SELECTED WRITINGS, SHEARSMAN EDITION

OTHER POETRY
Double Flute
Learning to Talk
Half of Nowhere
Against Perfection
Book With No Back Cover

PROSE
Keys to Transformation: Ceri Richards and Dylan Thomas
Imagems 1

AS EDITOR
An Octave for Octavio Paz
Ceri Richards : Drawings to Poems by Dylan Thomas
Rivers of Life
In Visible Ink : Selected Poems, Roberto Sanesi 1955-1979
Homage to Mandelstam
Out of Yugoslavia
For Angus
The Perfect Order: Selected Poems, Nasos Vayenas, 1974-2010

RICHARD BERENGARTEN

李道

CHANGING

WITH A PREFACE BY
EDWARD L. SHAUGHNESSY
夏含夷

AND CALLIGRAPHY BY
YU MINGQUAN
于明诠

Shearsman Books

This edition published in the United Kingdom in 2016
by Shearsman Books Ltd
50 Westons Hill Drive
Emersons Green
BRISTOL
BS16 7DF

Shearsman Books Ltd Registered Office
30–31 St. James Place, Mangotsfield, Bristol BS16 9JB
(this address not for correspondence)

www.shearsman.com

ISBN 978-1-84861-507-6

Contents

Edward L. Shaughnessy

Preface

The locusts' wings abuzz abuzz:
Properly made for progeny,
Praying that they will find a cause.

The locusts' wings sound and resound:
Properly made for progeny,
Predicting that their purpose be found.

The locusts' wings stirring a cloud:
Properly made for progeny,
Would that they read this poem aloud.
        (inspired by the poem 'Locusts'
Zhong si 螽斯] of China's *Classic of Poetry*)

I beg the reader's indulgence for beginning this Preface to Richard Berengarten's splendid new collection of poetry *Changing* with a poem of my own. I have no intention of competing with Berengarten in terms of literary merit. The reader will soon turn to *Changing* and will find that this collection of poems – or perhaps I should say, this single long poem, composed of many parts – easily withstands even an affront such as this. He has invited me to write this Preface so that I might say something about China's *Classic of Changes*, which has inspired his work.

Many readers will know of the *Changes* as the *I Ching* (regardless of how it might be pronounced) and will know both that it is the first of the Chinese classics and also that it began its existence as a divination manual. They probably will not think of it as poetry, except in the loosest of senses. *Changing* will certainly change that.

As indicated above, my little poem is inspired by the *Classic of Poetry* poem 'Locusts.' As does that poem, and many other poems of the *Classic of Poetry*, it features three stanzas that repeat incrementally, changing only the rhyme words. Each stanza begins with an image drawn from the natural world, and then goes on to relate this image to a topic in the human realm, the rhyme words driving the poem's development toward a desired conclusion. This three-stanza structure allows me to introduce a relationship between prayer, prophecy, and poetry, which I propose to explore a little further by way of preface to *Changing*. Many readers may recall the divine inspiration Plato attributed to poets. In the *Ion*, he compared poets to "diviners and holy prophets" as people who speak the words of god.

> God takes away the minds of poets, and uses them as his minis-
> ters, as he also uses diviners and holy prophets, in order that we
> who hear them may know them to be speaking not of themselves
> who utter these priceless words in a state of unconsciousness,
> but that god himself is the speaker, and that through them he is
> conversing with us.
>
> Plato, *Ion*

Changing provides us reason to hope that it was not only in antiquity that the gods spoke through the poets – as also the diviners and holy prophets – but that they may continue to do so today.

Having had the temerity to quote Plato, let me hasten to retreat to my role as a student of ancient China and hope that I can find support there for my understanding of Richard Berengarten's *Changing*. One of the unusual features of the Chinese language is that verbs of communication were originally bidirectional. "Buy" and "sell" were both written with the same word and may even have been pronounced the same, as were also "give" and "take," "explain" and "understand," "offer" and "enjoy," and countless other such words. Still today in modern Chinese "lend" and "borrow" are expressed with the same word, the direction of the transaction determining its sense. I do not wish to turn this Preface into a lesson in Chinese grammar, but it seems to me worth considering the bidirectionality of communication when we read Plato on poetry and divination. The gods speak to us through the poets, diviners and holy prophets, but the poets, diviners and holy prophets also speak to the gods for us. Some of the words they utter may be "in a state of unconsciousness," but other words are uttered in a state of full consciousness. Our poems and our prophecies are also our prayers.

Before going on to consider the *I Ching* or *Classic of Changes*, let me return briefly to China's *Classic of Poetry*, a younger sister to the *Classic of Changes*. The poem in that collection immediately following 'Locusts,' which inspired my own little poem at the beginning of this Preface, is en-titled 'The Peach Hangs Heavy' (*Tao yao* 桃夭). This time let me simply translate the poem (and do so without attempting to replicate the rhyme scheme, which would rhyme on the last word of each couplet).

Heavy hanging is the peach tree, Glistening fresh are its blossoms.
This is the girl going to marry, Fit and proper for house and home.

Heavy hanging is the peach tree, Ripely swollen is its fruit.
This is the girl going to marry, Fit and proper for home and house.

Heavy hanging is the peach tree, Its leaves thickly enveloping.
This is the girl going to marry, Fit and proper for home and man.

桃之夭夭，灼灼其華。之子于歸，宜其室家。
桃之夭夭，有蕡其實。之子于歸，宜其家室。
桃之夭夭，其葉蓁蓁。之子于歸，宜其家人。

It is easy enough to see that this is a simple wedding song, employing the image of a peach tree to suggest the success of the wedding. The glistening freshness of the peach blossoms attracts us to the girl, while the shape of the fruit surely predicts the swollen belly that the singers hoped she would soon have. If the symbolism of the enveloping leaves is perhaps less immediately intelligible, a walk through any peach grove would quickly show that the leaves of the peach tree wrap around the fruit, protecting the peach until it is mature enough to separate from the tree. Surely we are to see in this envelopment the mother protecting her "home," which is to say her children.

I think it is also easy to see that this poem is simultaneously a prayer and a prediction. Sung as the girl was going to her wedding, the singers were not just congratulating her, but praying that she would be fertile, and indeed through their song helping to ensure that she would be so. On the other hand, we know that not all prayers are answered, and not all weddings are successful. One of the most poetic lines of the *Classic of Changes* vividly evokes the emptiness of marital failure. The top line of *Gui mei* 歸妹 hexagram (#54), the name of which can mean either the "marrying maiden" or the "returning (i.e., divorcing) maiden" – another example of the bidirectionality of Chinese verbs of communication – reads:

The woman raises the basket: no fruit;
The man stabs the sheep: no blood.
There is nothing beneficial.

女承筐无實，士刲羊无血。无攸利。

Perhaps the image of a man stabbing sheep is distant from contemporary man's everyday life (though most of us could easily understand the significance of there being "no blood"). For a modern adaptation inspired by this line, Berengarten offers the following poem:

6. Her sudden mood switches

Her sudden mood switches,
in his eyes for no apparent
reason, but always in hers

his fault, locked him out
of her bed and, eventually
numbed his mind when-

ever he was in the house
at the same time as her. So
if she was in he went out

and vice-versa. When her
complaints about him boiled,
she said he never saw her

for herself, only for what
he could get out of her or
use her for. And he never

took a blind bit of notice
of what she really was, felt,
thought, believed, wanted.

Berengarten has taken more than a blind bit of notice, and through him we are able to feel, think, believe and want.

In China, the *Classic of Changes* is thought to encompass every aspect of human experience, from the beginning and end of heaven and earth back to the beginning again. True to its title, Richard Berengarten's *Changing* is similarly all-encompassing, with 450 poems corresponding to the six lines of the 64 hexagrams of the *Classic of Changes*, each poem changing perspective with each line, with each page. As is true of the hexagram and line statements of the *Classic of Changes*, these individual pieces also display various modes of correspondence, some related by content, some by form, and some by other more oblique links.

Disregarding for the moment the first two suites of poems, corresponding to the hexagrams *Qian* 乾, translated by Berengarten as 'Initiating,' and *Kun* 坤, 'Responding, Corresponding,' I propose to look at just two lines in the next hexagram, *Zhun* 屯, 'Beginning,' usually a good place to begin. It may not be a coincidence that the second line of this hexagram contains an oracle involving birth. In my own translation, it reads as follows:

> Six in the Second: Stick-stuck, carts and horses lined up. Not bandits in marriage relations. Determining about a woman not pregnant, in ten years she is pregnant.

> 六二：屯如邅如，乘馬班如。匪寇，婚媾。女子貞不字，十年乃字。

This has inspired the following beautiful poem in *Changing*:

2. Hearing the other smiling

I'm pregnant,
she told her mother on
her (mother's) birthday.

After her first scan
she phoned and said
It's two and a half

centimetres long
and I can hear its
heart beat.

Where are you?
Asked her mother. I'm
In the car. I've

Just come out of
the clinic. In and through
the silence at each

end of the line
both women heard
the other smiling.

Not all of the line statements of *Zhun* hexagram similarly concern birth and beginnings. The third line statement changes perspective entirely to take us into the forest.

> Six in the Third: Approaching a deer without hunting: It is entering into the forest's midst, The nobleman might just as well let it go. Going: distress.

六三：即鹿无虞：惟入于林中，君子幾不如舍。往吝。

This has in its turn inspired Berengarten to offer the following poem:

> 3. A doe
>
> With his father's
> gun he shot a doe
> in the wood.
>
> The creature, eyes
> misting over, lay on
> her side, quivering
>
> as organs gave
> out and blood gushed
> from the wound.
>
> The boy approached
> the animal's
> supine head
>
> and stroked
> her in wonder.
> Then, as if in
>
> gratitude,
> she licked his
> proferred hand.

As one might expect, in the long Chinese involvement with the *Classic of Changes* there is some precedence for finding poetic inspiration in its hexagram and line statements. Best known of these is the *Yi lin* 易林 or *Forest of Changes* of Jiao Gan焦贛, better known as Jiao Yanshou 焦延壽, who lived in the middle of the first century B.C. Unfortunately, the *Forest of Changes* is one of only a few early Chinese texts that has never been translated; for this reason, even among Western aficionados of the *Changes*, it remains almost unknown. Whereas Richard Berengarten offers us 450 poems inspired by the line statements of the *Changes*, the *Forest of Changes* includes 4,096 poems, sixty-four for each of the sixty-four hexagrams, beginning with a single hexagram and then cycling through all of the other sixty-three hexagrams in turn. That the *Forest of Changes* remains untranslated may be due as much to the more or less hackneyed nature of most of its poetry as it is to its great length. The poems are largely composed of images drawn from the *Classic of Poetry* with occasional nods to Han-Dynasty politics. Nevertheless, the text deserves to be better known. Here I offer translations of just the first eight poems inspired by Zhun hexagram.

'Beginning' (*Zhun*, #3)
The troops attacking Ferghana, Going out north through the Jade Gate.
Battling against the Hun bandits, Bringing peace west of the city road.
In seven days their food cut off, Hardly able to keep self whole.

屯、兵征大宛，北出玉關。與胡寇戰，平城道西，七日絕糧，身幾不全。

Its 'Initiating' (*Qian*, #1)
Drifting, drifting the cypress boat, Floating along without stopping.
Wracked and worried wide awake, The heart full of anxiety.
When goodness doesn't meet its time, Return to live in the shadows.

乾、汎汎柏舟，流行不休。耿耿寤寐，心懷大憂。仁不逢時，復隱窮居。

Its 'Responding' (*Kun*, #2)

Gath'ring firewood getting a *lin*, The great mandate falls upside down.
The heroes all battling for fame, The world divided every which way.

坤、採薪得麟，大命隕顛。豪雄爭名，天下四分。

Its 'Bringing Up' (*Meng*, #4)
Mountains toppled valleys cut off, Heaven's blessings are all used up.
The Jing and Wei run out of course, The Jade Registry at an end.

蒙、山崩谷絕，天福盡竭。涇渭失紀，玉厤盡已。

Its 'Waiting' (*Xu*, #5)
The Summer Terrace and Youli, Where Tang and Wen were put in jail.
The Lord of Ghosts sent in a bribe, So the Shang king then set him free.

需、夏臺羑里，湯、文所厄。鬼侯俞賄，商王解舍。

Its 'Clashing' (*Song*, #6)
The muddy ford dirties honor, Thrown away into the ditch.
Held up to laughter and to tears, In the end there is no reward.

訟、泥津汙辱，棄捐溝瀆。所共笑哭，終不顯錄。

Its 'Mustering' (*Shi*, #7)
Pears and plums fruit in the winter, The country full of bandits and thieves.
Turmoil and chaos all around, The ruler unable to rest.

師、李梅冬實，國多盜賊。擾亂並作，君不能息。

Its 'Binding' (*Bi*, #8)
The does and bucks chased to the wilds, Eating their fill return to home.
Turning back as far as the hut, There is nothing to make you sick.

比、獐鹿逐牧，飽歸其居。反還次舍，無有疾故。

Although Jiao Yanshou was renowned in his day for his ability to use the *Changes* to predict the future, it is hard to fathom the oracles at work in these poems. They seem to exist largely out of time, and indeed have long been suspected of being later forgeries. However, the most recent manuscript discovery out of China suggests that Jiao Yanshou was also drawing on a contemporary tradition that presented poetic prophecies. In early 2009, Peking University received a gift of a cache of bamboo-strip manuscripts that apparently had recently been looted from a Han-Dynasty tomb. In 2013, the first of these manuscripts was published: a Han-Dynasty copy of the *Laozi* 老子, also known as the *Dao de jing* 道德經 or *Classic of the Way and Virtue*, though this manuscript – like the famous Mawangdui 馬王堆 manuscript before it, would better be titled the *Classic of Virtue and the Way* since it reverses the two major sections of the text.

In late 2015, the university published a second volume of manuscripts, this one including a previously unknown text entitled *Jing jue* 荊決 or *Jing Decisions*, Jing 荊 referring to the important southern state of *Chu* 楚 by its alternate name, and "decisions" referring to divination consultations. The text presents a different method of sorting milfoil stalks from that used by the *Classic of Changes*, counting through thirty stalks to produce a result made up of just three lines, the top and bottom lines of which are drawn horizontally, while the middle line is drawn vertically. The text begins by describing the method of sorting the stalks:

> Drilling the turtle and announcing to the milfoil is not as good as 'Jing Decisions.' Whether yin or yang, whether long or short, what is divined has no limit, what is prognosticated has nothing better; one must examine it with clarity. Thirty stalks are used to divine its affairs, whether lucky or ominous, only the stalks are to be followed. In the left hand holding the document, in the right hand holding the stalks, one must face to the east. Using thirty stalks, divide them into three groups; the upper is horizontal, the middle group is vertical, the bottom group is horizontal. Discard them four by four, but what is not full is not to be discarded.

There then follow sixteen different oracles, correlated with different days and different results. Here I will present just two representative oracles.

Yi 乙 (#2):
The dragon dwelling in the marsh, wishing to rise into heaven.
A lucky day, a happy hour, rise on high and scan the distance,
Examine it by the color.
As for today what day is it? Lucky and joyous unlimited.
The ford's bridge having been travelled, one's wishes hit the intention.
Lucky, the external is the demon.

龍處于澤，欲登于天。吉日嘉時，登高曲望，相焉以
色。今日何日，吉樂無極。。津橋氣行，願欲中意。
吉，外屬祟。

Gui 癸 (#10):
The black bird in the morning flies, soaring-soaring kingfisher
wings.
Traveling together with another, his body located all alone.
Requests for audience say yes, But there are wishes not approved.
As for today, what day is it: a lucky man about to come.
Day in night out watching for him, hoping his coming meets
the date.
Lucky, the demons are one's grandfather and grandmother,
Minor Lucky.

玄鳥朝蜇（飛），羊羊翠羽。與人皆行，其身蜀處。請
謁云若，有欲弗許。今日何日，吉人將來。日【夜望
之】，責來會期。吉，祟王父母，【小吉】。

As do the poems of the *Forest of Changes*, the oracles of the *Jing Decisions* adapt images that had first appeared in the *Classic of Changes* and the *Classic of Poetry* almost a thousand years earlier and combine them with topical references to daily life in the Han dynasty to predict something of the future. Even better than the *Forest of Changes*, these oracles might be said to be what Plato was describing as the inspired utterances of poets, diviners and holy prophets. Now, two thousand years later and in a very different part of the world, Richard Berengarten has drawn inspiration once again from the *Changes* to give us 450 poems—or, perhaps otherwise considered, one single poem in 450 sections—that once again refresh these ancient images.

In closing, let me note that one unique feature of the *Classic of Changes* is that while its penultimate hexagram is entitled *Jiji* 既濟 or

'After Crossing Over' (in other words, 'Already Completed'), its sixty-fourth and final hexagram is *Weiji* 未濟 or 'Before Crossing Over' ('Not Yet Completed'). One implication of this is that when you think you are about to be finished, you realize that you have just begun. Another, slightly different implication is that one ending is but another beginning. That is the nature of change and changing. It is time to end this preface and begin *Changing*. To begin at almost the end, here is the hexagram statement of 'Before Crossing Over' hexagram as well as Richard Berengarten's poem inspired by it. 'No harm done. Not yet.' Indeed.

> Before Crossing Over: Receipt. The little fox at the point of crossing, wets his tail. There is no place beneficial.

《未濟》亨。小狐汔濟，濡其尾，无攸利。

Fire-tail

Fox, little fire-tail, not
really ready to cross such a
broad flooded river, not

yet big or strong enough
for this biggest test of all,
now you've trodden a

fine fierce line between
moving forward bravely,
sensibly, carefully, and

taking a fat reckless
plunge, gambling, getting
in over your head. Never

mind, there'll be more
chances later, to try again
when you're a bit more

savvy, stronger, and
waters aren't so full. No
harm done. Not yet.

道可道非常道

* * *

Μεταβάλλον ἀναπαύεται.

* * *

Omnia in omnibus & singula in singulis.

* * *

There are more things in heaven and earth, Horatio,
Than are dreamt of in your philosophy.

* * *

All the world is full of inscape and chance left
free to act falls into an order as well as purpose.

* * *

Un coup de dés jamais n'abolira le hasard

* * *

The song would speak
Of that interminable building reared
By observation of affinities
In objects where no brotherhood exists
To passive minds.

* * *

so lag mir der Gedanke nahe, mir das Buch gewissermassen
als Person vorzustellen und an diese die Frage zu richten

* * *

un système où tout se tient

* * *

αὐτὸς ὁ κόσμος δὲν εἶναι ὁ δικός μας, εἶναι τοῦ Ὁμήρου

* * *

it coheres all right

* * *

Initiating

heaven over heaven   *heaven under heaven*

Heaven

Heaven over heavens
heaven under heavens
when and where do

you ever stop? Breath
fails, mind can't conceive
your blazing blackness

your white dark
your black brilliance
your inhering glory

your endlessness
in beginninglessness
each in each other

beauty-filled
wisdom-filled
universe

nothing everything
destroying generating
everything nothing

元 *sublime*　　亨 *accomplish*　　利 *further*　　貞 *persevere*

1. Bending light

Stars pull and bend
light like archers. Which our
astronomers claim holds

good in all wherewhens.
As I lie in bed pondering this,
a nocturnal cat climbs

a willow onto my shallow-
sloped roof. What things we
may see up there, roof-cat

and I, are events' shards
objects no longer occupy.
The further we gaze, the

further we peer back. Pushed
and pulled by gravities, things
tumbling eventfully across

skies eventually whirl
into nothings, into holes of
sheer nothing.

2. What Zhang Zai thought

Out walking alone as an autumn
sun was going down and a yellow ball
of a hunter's moon coming up,

Zhang Zai sat on a tree stump
and quietly forgot about time and
mortality and himself awhile

as he soaked himself into
and through things. Not much of
a life, he thought, if you can't

or don't get a chance to see
patterns and images of heaven
and earth as merely sediment

of marvellous transformations.
And not much of a view if you've
forgotten it. Better be poor and

remember this than have power
and wealth and forget heaven is
text and context for all wisdom.

dragon   *rising in the field*

3. Cohering, inhering

All day long and
all night long it starts
now now. To

keep everything
(every *thing*) in mind
in its entirety, and

still focus entire on
this? As the universe
keeps all measures

and all in measure,
and each thing main-
tains its own seams,

stains, marks, patterns,
edges, pleats, horizons –
may the same quiet

patient appetite for
order cohere, inhere
in this, in here.

4. Oscillating

From endless
beginninglessness, dawnless
and duskless

energy arises
forming and informing *this*
whose matter and

pattern arose, arises
and will arise – and sank
and sinks and will

sink again. From
nothing oneness both
one and the same

and from oneness
two then one then nothing.
This constant flow

between *notness*
and *isness* becomes and is
all ways key.

5. Absolute

Absolute beginning
and final end of all ends
and beginnings

'behind' space-time
clasp tight together, as
one, indissoluble –

as hands open
in greeting, as a bracelet
bands a wrist, as gems

encrust a necklace, as
a crown sets on a head,
as hair fastens in skin,

as concentric light-
domes surround living
trees, as angles and

sides of an egg –
incessantly changing
yet changeless.

6. Light fills and fails

Light fills and fails. It hovers, spills away.
Dark narrows path and yard. Night smothers field.
How foil this overflow? How stall the day?

Out there, against the cliffs, beyond the bay,
a ship is sinking, caving in, unkeeled.
Light fills and fails. It hovers, spills away.

The mast has split in two beneath salt spray.
Crushed like an egg, it sinks. Its sides must yield.
How foil this overflow? How stall the day?

No hoop of faith or stave of hope can stay
the chaos that this dark flood has unsealed.
Light fills and fails. It hovers, spills away.

Our ground itself unhinges. Rock, mud, clay
swirl as vast spools of shadow are unreeled.
How foil this overflow? How stall the day?

Terror has been unleashed. We're easy prey
to swirling hordes of phantoms day concealed.
Light fills and fails. It hovers, spills away.
How foil this overflow? How stall the day?

powerful dragon   *meets his match*

☯ Supreme Ultimate

Endless beginningless
heaven holds everything
including astronomical

creation and demise
of universes into and out
of nothing. How

many dimensions can
you imagine? Well, heaven
has more, folding in

and out of one
another, replicating,
self-swallowing,

interbreeding. In this
part-perceived and part-
undiscovered cosmos

lie still and always
more unemptiable fecund
sources overspilling.

(2)

Responding, Corresponding

earth above earth   *earth beneath earth*

Earth

You paradisal particle of star
you panoramic green and yellow maze
you mother of particularities

you centre folding in upon yourself
with cloudy blue and grey circumference
unfallen and revolving around fire

you crusted ball of lava balanced on
one invisible axis, indiscernible strings
keeping your modest place, your

rolling pace, as doing nothing, you
revolve and spin – you tabulated Eden
terrible and wonderful and ordinary

you grounder of primordial glory
which you absorb and increase billionfolds
in every-each inseparable moment

you seething and proliferating surface
you forested and river-fed and windblown
time-space of human origins and ends

元 *spring*   亨 *summer*   利 *autumn*   贞 *winter*

1. Fields frost

Fields frost. So no talk
now of rest or sleep. That
dour music is the wind

blowing down from
northern deserts. Not even
rats peep out. Now we

follow season as guide
and master. Soon snows
will arrive, last all winter.

You think this place
paradise? Perfect gardens
need patient cultivation.

So fetch buckets. Boil
water from broken ice.
Put on lined boots and

gloves. Start chopping.
Keep blocks dry. Light
slow smouldering fire.

---

frost underfoot   *ice will come*

2. Walking, in a garden

The flower's scent spills.
The bee, its instrument, pursues
its destiny. Aware how

beauty's song pierces
this quiet, how could I fault such
treasure, such abundance?

All summer long I shall
stay here and be – this being just
what being is and for,

when nothing left or else need
be pursued – *this* also being when
this garden thrusts

its whole sustaining glory out –
so richly I breathe summer in entire
as summer breathes me also in

itself. Flowers' scents, spilling,
track and trawl their bees. Each
instrument obeys its destiny.

---

effortless   *in motion, spontaneous*

3. Change

How shall changes
let alone Change itself
be understood and

measured? The one
immeasurable law that
governs all things, at

least in this universe,
is that everything every-
where is constantly

on the move through-
out spacetime, just as
reciprocally spacetime

itself is always on
the move through
things. The one

common inhering
condition that never
changes is Change.

---

excellence, hidden   *discovered when the time is ripe*

4. Tie up a bag

I looked down in my bag
of selves and made *this*. It
wasn't enough. It never is.

I opened up pockets in
bags in bags. I breathed
in and out of them, and

with, from, through them.
I waited without waiting, ab-
sorbing whatever lay

ready, already, here. But
what found its way here
wasn't what I saw

thanks to my bags, but
what saw and found me. All
I had sewn I unsewed, to

get it right as could-be,
no longer bothering with
bags, pockets or an *I*.

to tie words and actions   *in cloth of caution*

5. A yellow lower garment

This light playing
swaying, straying, spraying
across these

clouded hills, over
these pleasant flowing
waters – so palpable

you could almost
touch it, though you
know it can't be

caught, how ever it may
streak, stroke, strike you –
light one and all,

all one, everywhere –
yes, you flow and cohere
all right, very right,

as do these notes, in
white light, black light,
alternating, oscillating.

can'st 'ou see   *with the eyes of turquoise*

6. The force that fills and empties

The force that fills and empties things of day
and straddles stars with particles and waves,
holds all our love, yet wipes that love away.

See, night's obsidian floors in rich array
lie strewn with light. Each single one engraves
the force that fills and empties things of day.

Stirring breath, blood and bones, it spurs my clay
to build the buttresses and architraves
that hold our love, yet wipes it clean away.

While all things pass, and children run and play,
each atom matter holds connected paves
the force that fills and empties things of day.

Staining the sky in blue, and the blue bay,
sifting clear waters into rills and caves,
it holds our love, yet wipes that love away.

Come, friend, sit with me. Drink this wine, I pray,
and break bread, though around us chaos raves.
The force that fills and empties things of day
holds all our love, yet wipes that love away.

dragons fighting   *across wild skies*

7. Being simple

This is where we start
every time – in purposeless
potential, in a *before* so far

'back' 'behind' all other
befores, it can't really be counted
as being *in* time of any kind,

let alone pertaining to or
belonging to time. Its *isness* –
meshed so tight and sheer

into its *notness* that neither
is extricable from the other –
yields a pointless point

neither passive nor active,
neither *this* nor *that* but both –
point of departure and

eternal return – and if an
image at all, then one that is
not-an-image, a not-image.

unhewn block   樸   *uncarved wood*

(3)

Beginning

---

thunder thickens   *below cloud cluster*

Seed, seeding, seedling

Thunder topped by down-
pour. A seed hardly visible to
human eyes swells, splits,

opens, pushes up and down,
down and up, powered in each
and every one of its expansive

nano-changes by latent pre-
patterned responses to chemical-
physical signals and triggers –

primed, ready, waiting, ripe
for particular sets of factors
to co-occur – so that it may

become, be, live. Pausing to
register this, how can one not
be stunned by the ordinary

extraordinary miraculousness
of this epiphany, this thisness,
this entire matter of living?

heaven   *in a wild flower*

1. January-end already

January-end already. But
she hasn't yet caught up even
with this year's beginning,

is still stuck in last year
and deaths of two friends
haunt her. Sickness

of spirit weighs on her
binding her in coughing fits
and repeated bad dreams.

So come in, come on,
new-old year (she says), I want
to jump in you right now, as

if you were a water-pool,
a long-held note, a spring
wind on a Japanese

mountain, a market
in a warm country, a new
world I don't recognise.

---

considering, lingering   *hesitating, hindering*

2. Hearing the other smiling

I'm pregnant,
she told her mother on
her (mother's) birthday.

After her first scan
she phoned and said
It's two and a half

centimetres long
and I can hear its
heart beat.

Where are you?
asked her mother. I'm
in the car. I've

just come out of
the clinic. In and through
the silence at each

end of the line
both women heard
the other smiling.

---

after ten years   *she conceives*

3. A doe

With his father's
gun he shot a doe
in the wood.

The creature, eyes
misting over, lay on
her side, quivering

as organs gave
out and blood gushed
from the wound.

The boy approached
the animal's
supine head

and stroked
her in wonder.
Then, as if in

gratitude,
she licked his
proffered hand.

chasing deer, no guide   *let flee, humiliation*

4. Street urchin, dancing

Acrobatic, Puck-like,
a small boy has jumped
with flexed knees

onto my shoulders
in one leap. He lands per-
fectly, and laughs.

Jolted, I take one step
back. I almost want to
thank him that we're

joined – me, piggy, and
he, child-rider. Me, a kind
of father, and he 'my'

infant son? Now I
laugh too. No more tests.
No more judgements.

More children of all
ages arrive. Everyone
romps and cavorts.

---

shouldering a shadow   *move on*

5. For a very small child

Hushabye and close
your eyes and breathe
gently now because

the ant's strong legs
will bear you into sleep,
the back of a butterfly

transport you and
breath of a bird blow
you high and away

to dreamland where
you'll roll on a cloud
then fall and tumble

safe down a raindrop
onto the glossy blade of
a hart's tongue fern

and there you'll
slumber till morning peels
away night's drapes.

6. Biding (his) time

The entire national economy has
cracked up. He has a job and works
hard but doesn't get paid. Nobody

who works for a public institution
gets paid. The whole country is in debt.
Nearly everyone in it is in debt too.

This isn't his time or anyone else's.
In the capital students and workers
demonstrate outside parliament.

With bare hands they tear down
walls. Pull up flagstones. Hoist parked
cars on top. Then torch the piles.

Screaming behind barricades they
hurl missiles. Police disperse rioters
with tear gas. He, meanwhile, stays

at home in his provincial town.
Borrows money. Tightens his belt.
Goes on working. Bides his time.

ready but not going forward   *how long can it last*

(4)

Bringing up

a stream   *under a mountain*

Child, counting

Wind keeps counting
sandgrains on shifting dunes.
He cannot count me.

Summer keeps counting
stars in clear night skies.
He cannot count me.

Storm keeps counting
rain pellets in her heart.
She cannot count me.

Light keeps counting
things. She won't ever stop.
She cannot count me.

Death keeps counting
hordes of sparrows and starlings,
hairs on your head, and

bare bones on heaps. But
I'm hiding behind closed fingers.
He cannot count me.

---

a spring   *flows out of a mountain*

1. Himself at the centre

The project that term
was c o m m u n I t y. The boy
was asked to draw

himself at the centre
then radiate lines out to all
things he was part of.

So first he drew a building
with himself and his family
in it and he wrote h o m e.

Then he drew another
and wrote s c h o o l. His teacher
had explained r e l i g i o n,

so, aiming to please her,
easily he sketched a t e m p l e.
Then he wrote f o o t b a l l,

adding a picture. Now
he was at a loss. What
else did he belong to?

2. In the primary school

In the primary school poetry
workshop a nine-year old boy
called Shane stood up and

read the poem he'd been
making. As he stopped a hush
swept through the eighty

or so children of his age
sitting on the polished wooden
floor in the assembly hall.

And in that silence we
were held in an almost palpable
ring of awe, made by

Shane's words rippling
on and through air into our
ears, until one child

put hands together
and started clapping and
everyone joined in.

3. Dependence, veiled

Liz listens or, rather, seems
to listen to you so attentively,
hanging on your every word

as she cocks her small head
sideways, fluttering eyelashes,
cutely adding a smile, plus

the *soupçon* of a pout, well
practised before her mirror –
she can hardly fail to pull

you closer, ever closer, as
you scent her sweet helplessness,
her ready receptive warmth.

Fall for her and you'll lose
your heart, mind, and more.
Though you may be a man

of steel, to her you're no
more than a stepping stone
to her dream man of gold.

---

a shallow river, shadowed   *dangerous*

4. Carollers, scruffy kids

Unbroken voices, raucous, weeks
before Christmas tidings of comfort
and cheer – they banged hard on

our knocker to scream cynical
carols at us. We sent them packing
with nothing and no thanks. Now

it's New Year and the scruffy
kids bang on our knocker harder
every evening and run off

into dusk around the corner
up the street past the pub into
the alley before we can get to

our front door. Sometimes they
stuff squashed rotten tangerines
and banana skins through our

letter box. They're quick as
pixies on their feet and we don't
know who their parents are.

will they or we   *work it out*

5. Child, calculating

If I step on slabs
not on cracks between
Tiger won't get me.

If Counter-Woman won't
turn before I get my purse out
Snake won't get me.

If I reach Red Gate before
I've counted seventy-seven
T. Rex won't get me.

If I don't go back and pick up
the bag I chucked in the gutter
Ghoulie won't get me.

If I pretend I'm asleep
and they don't see I'm not
Skeleton won't get me

If I count more than 14
and under 17 cherry stones
I'll be all right.

6. Samuel Brighteyes

Here comes Samuel Bright-
eyes sauntering down my street
in blossom-spattered May.

Who taught him to do
that wasn't me. He materialises
from haze, he self-clarifies,

sleek hair parted over one
brow, mischievous sparky eyes,
bony long-nailed fingers,

cleft chin, dimples, pink
cheeks, puckering smile, and
scruffy old-man-little-boy

wise-wizened complexion.
He faces me with penetrating
ice-blue eyes. We size each

other up. We shake hands.
I pull him tight towards me.
We hug. Both of us laugh.

delinquent   _recalcitrant_

(5)

Waiting, Needing

---

cloud   *covering heaven*

Against clouds

Wind's invisible fingers
carved drypoint letters on
a beech tree's leaves.

Foliage's scratchmarks,
blurred against clouds, lay
twisted face up on sky.

Then wind's puckered
mouth spread hints of
almost-words through

the tree's entire body,
reiterating them with
each renewed gust.

Then wind dissolved,
letting leaves speak to
themselves, without

thanking its disposers,
three parts dropletted,
four parts ash.

under thunder, waiting   watching the kingdom's brilliance

1. Ordinary

Outwardly lacking an I,
though being all eye, with
head low, he stands

in line among others,
a morsel, mere wheel-cog,
back-of-chorus member,

an innocuous, guileless
particle in an average non-
threatening wave among

countless other waves –
face apparently readable,
posing no hint of danger.

By not being noticed,
he has fuller chance of
survival. So he waits

on outskirts for
time when his time may
come or might come

in need, waiting   *at the edges*

2. In the desert (1)

Deserts have no corners
only edges. Ridge, ledge, crest –
border of blurred horizon

where degree of slippage
correlates with enormities of
brandished, burnished

silence – except for wind
and our animals rolling with it
and sand swishing beneath.

What do you want? asked
my guide, meaning: That isn't
the way to go. And she pulled

her veil across her eyes and
faced into the wind. What's
to be seen, she added, isn't

all that's to be reckoned.
Neither visible nor unseen
ever stops changing.

in need, waiting   *in yellow brightness*

3. Mists

Word sentinels loom
megalithic among swirling
mists of many meanings

under this murderous
sky. Out of these bubbling
hazes mixed of mud,

dream-maze and longing,
they tower and lower and
call out. Indeed 'me'

they call and call
out to follow them and
make these. Some

crumble and others
won't get through but
some will break

or sneak their ways
over, through and past
ever-insistent death.

4. Aged 21

Cellars she had to spend
seven years of nights in, to
enter adulthood, were set

in mountains of compacted
betrayals – Africa by Europe,
Jews and Gypsies by Nazis,

Pygmies and Aborigines
by British. Ancestral spirits
lurking on buried edges

of barbaric atrocities, she
confronted in her nightmares
by breathing quietly

and keeping as still as
she could, while watching
inwards and outwards

simultaneously. Never
again would she let insight be
bought by others' suffering.

---

in need, waiting   *to get out of the ditch*

5. A reading of now

A reading of now
and its tails and hooks
antennae and entrails

roots and routes
tendrils and crannies
webs and branches

ropes and plaitings
longings and hopes
coils and pleats

curlings and closures
alleyways and byways
sources and estuaries

questions and quests
imminent and immanent
pitfalls and strands

and movements of
this to its ends here is
posited, is posted.

6. Transparencies

The girl under the black umbrella
picks her nose with her free hand.
Three buses go by. Not one stops.

Everything in this shop costs a
pound. Nothing is worth it. Crows
nest on chimney stacks at numbers

27 & 29 Stockwell St. Their cackle
is a racket. They shit on parked cars.
Our stoop-shouldered regular raver

does his daily neighbourhood round.
'Fuck Bin Laden,' he yells. 'Fuck Bush.
Fuck Blair. Fuck Brown.' Adding for

good measure, 'Fuck the Pope.' A
young mother wheels her dozy toddler
round the corner in a pink buggy.

Our ranter smiles and stops yelling
until she has walked past. He peeks
cockeyed at the railway bridge.

---

down in the pits   *a guest, unexpected*

(6)

Clashing

---

heaven   *over water*

Judge and jury

Though fallible, the least dishonest
way to resolve disputes and punish
crimes remains through laws long

laid down, painstakingly modified
by continual re-testing against evidence
and re-interpretation to new and

unforeseen circumstances, applied
coolly and conscientiously, yet with
compassion by an impartial judge

alert and wise to all possible niceties,
facets, implications, loopholes and scams
in precedent, punishment, procedure

and relevant permissible interpretation
within code and constitution – working
with an independent unthreatened jury

formed of hopefully-not-indecent citizens –
unpaid laymen and laywomen sworn to
determine and deliver unbiased verdict.

---

mid-point alone is correct 中 *pivot, fulcrum*

1. Jasper and Jonas

Jasper accused Jonas
and Jonas Jasper of da-
maging a wall joining

their estates – wrangle
swollen into self-righteous
posturing, mutual blame,

insult, abuse and re-
fusal to examine shadows
lying under motive.

Judge Julius ruled Jasper
and Jonas would share costs
equally, appointed an

arbitrator, and ordered
both claimants to abide by
his decision. Pursuing

one's own cause alone
will end badly. Better stop,
conciliate, move on.

2. Jaabir

In a fenny village, a gang
of lads sets on the swarthy
stranger, taunting him

with street names. So Jaabir
pulls out an airgun, waves it,
and they call the police

who evict him. Pale-skinned
farmers' boys, their ways are
supported by bye-laws.

It might be best to go
home, if he had or could
choose one, or afford

to pay his way back.
As it is, any possible home
must be here, in this fine

hospitable country, which
he entered in peace and hope
to work to earn to live in.

---

unable to wrangle, escape   *or go home*

3. Julius

Born into a family of loyal
sons of loyal sons, Julius followed
custom and expectation in

schooling, pastimes and
duties. Devoted, unquestioning
and unoriginal, irritating to

even his most conventional
friends, he turned out neither
yes-man nor pushover when

appointed to the bench
but delivered oddly imaginative
rulings, rooted in

precedent and, equally,
in compassion. Without trace of
pomposity or personal vanity

he upheld and passed on
values he deemed decent,
viable, honourable.

4. Jackson

With his boy-pranks verging
on malice, ringleader in revolt,
young Jackson challenged

custom and disobeyed
direct orders whenever he
possibly could. Then

triggered by no obvious
event, as if a disconnected
cog in his metabolism

had magically clicked into
place, Jackson directed all
his talents, focus, energies

into teaching. In old age,
he was loved and respected
in his neighbourhood

as an inspiring motivator
and innovator who always
did things his own way.

5. A treaty

The two sides made their
treaty by hard negotiation. It
wasn't easy. They stood for

factions who had hated each
other for more than 100 years
Hard-bitten old warriors

by the end were able to
see and respect humanity in
each other, even to share

a private meal, car journey,
handshake, public platform,
mild joke. Moving behind

scenes among both parties
in seclusion from public glare
teams of dedicated, inspired

moderators worked with
them for release of hostages
and sharing of territory.

dealing with contention   中道   *from the correct perspective*

6. A white horse

Master Ni Yue enjoyed
arguing a white horse isn't
a horse. Effortlessly he

argued strips off
all-comers. By alternately
confuting and separating

subcategory and kind
he ran rings around even
most sophisticated

intellectual adversaries
never failing to walk away
laughing. But when

Ni Yue rode through
West City Gate on his own
white horse, imperial

frontier guards, following
standard procedures, taxed
him. For owning a horse.

black belt in sophistry   *then demoted*

(7)

Mustering, Conscripting

Don't waste time

Joe Hill, aka Hillstrom,
born Joel Emmanuel Hägglund
7 Oct 1879, Gävle, Sweden,

having been set up and wrong-
fully accused of murder, died
19 Nov 1915, Utah – for

whom 36 was way too early
to die, having still exceedingly
much life in him, very

far to go, and masses left
to do, organizing migrants
and sweatshop workers

in the San Pedro Branch
of the Industrial Workers of
the World. The night before

he was executed, Joe telegraphed
Big Bill Haywood: 'Don't waste
time in mourning. Organize.'

---

one able to lead multitudes   might bring peace to the world

1. James Gibson remembers D Day

So they opened fire
on us from a ditch and we
returned it. And when

their firing stopped we
decided to take a peep.
We found nineteen of

them dead and one still
alive, moaning. When night
fell I said, I'm going to go

and sit with him. Don't,
they said. The bodies might
be boobied. But I went

anyway. He spoke good
English and I sat with him
till he died. He gave me

a set of photos and
asked me to send them
back to his family.

send out an army   *toss away lives*

2. In the spirit of Walt Whitman

It's villages and small
towns across the world
I'm interested in and

care for, not countries –
it's hamlets and their fields,
paddies, vineyards, orchards,

slopes, woods, forests,
pastures, grazing savannahs,
names of trees and fruits,

birds, animals, fish
in lakes, seas, rivers – their
habitations, movements –

buzz and flack of
weathers and winds, and
special sky-qualities –

dialects and tropes
of each unique *this*, familiar
to a person, to persons.

3. Emperor's army, freed

The Emperor's warriors
did not defend him from
all-powerful Death or

stop him being sent to the
Underworld but, buried with
him, stood guard for him,

sealed under deep-piled
dust and sand, a terracotta army,
life-sized, of 8000 men

as if ensouled – infantry,
cavalry, clay horses, chariots
unseen across twenty-two

centuries. Farmers plumbing
a well found a pit. Archaeologists
dug out thousands of warriors

and polished them one by one
like gods. In stilled ranks they
stand, diverse, individualised.

who is in charge   *of this army*

4. Emperor's army, captured

He who had burned books,
buried scholars and alchemists,
massacred hundreds of

thousands of workers, united
China, and begun building the Wall,
couldn't command or control

impervious Death. Unearthed
now, under daylight and nightlight,
his warriors stand guard

in ranks, massed as if alive.
Clay-fleshed, clay-armed, in
clay preserved, lacking

nothing but fleshed breath,
who now do they celebrate
most? Their Emperor or

Death, who has conquered
and captured them and parades
them as His prisoners?

5. Allow ceremonies

Poison casks are
unstoppered and revenge
floats free, frothing

deadliest on waves of
cornered murmurs. Those who
call themselves civilized

clench fists, grind teeth,
suffer headaches and, like
stage villains, screw up

eyes in hate. So allow
ceremonies and dirges. Do
not consign bones of your

enemy's son to dust by
some shack or hovel outside
his city's walls. Accord his

sisters, children, mother,
widow, dignity of a funeral
befitting kin of a man.

6. With equal honours

And bury them with equal
honours, your friend's son who fell,
whose father blessed your

youth with his elegance
and wit, fine athletic looks
and breathtaking ability to

unthink your own thoughts
even before you uttered them.
Equally, the only son of

your sworn longstanding
enemy, who in cold blood would
gladly have disposed of you

had you not outmanoeuvred
him by your own quicker cunning
that coaxed him into exile. Let

pallbearers carry both coffins
parallel in precedence. Walk behind
both, first among mourners.

taking charge   _bestow merit where it is due_

(8)

According, Binding

Listening to Schubert

She walks in here
on the wavering thread
of a violin's

longest note. The tide
is in and the bay ablaze
in sunset's wake,

waves flecked
crimson and violet and
honey and amber

and veridian and opal
and rose. Go then, song,
do not lose your tenuous

foothold. Stay alert
to clamber those invisible
boughs and towers

carved and engrained
in the ocean's endless
slopes and terraces.

1. As water

When you and I come together,
we join in a union, blend in a unity,
flow in a unison.

When you and I join together,
from no matter how far, as the song
says, 'across the wide prairie',

we are as one – indeed, *are* one –
just as light, in touching everything
when it cuts across dark,

adheres to things in its path, and
inheres within them too, inviolate –
and as water, which knows no

plurality, joining always itself,
seamlessly fills all lowest places
upwards. Sounded, fathomed

by eyes, breaths, hearts,
signed in words and silences,
bonds unbreakable.

2. Something and nothing

'Before any something, was
there a nothing? Or was there
a something else? If nothing

came first, wasn't that nothing
a something in its own *notness*, its
very *elseness*?' asked Duke Ai.

Zhuangzi said, 'Whether *thinghood*
came *out of notness,* of nothing else
or something else, how can I,

who know nothing about something
and nothing about nothing, possibly
tell the difference between the first

of all somethings and the very
first nothing? Skies pass and are
still and always sky. We, who

ask and watch, dream and
wake beneath them. Each one
of us, a something. A nothing.'

3. The third other

'And you and I together, by our
union itself, generate a third – not
that passing shadow who walks

at times beside one or other of us,
whom both have glimpsed through
curtained windows, in half-light,

hovering behind a chair, or
behind half-closed eyes, between
sleep and waking – but another

other, belonging to neither,
to neither one nor the other, formed
out of our *eachnesses*, our

isnesses, our *othernesses*,
our *bothnesses* – our selves –
an entirely separate being.

Once this third other arrives,
history begins. How many more
shall time and space allow?'

4. Still

'Substance and shadow belong to
each other. Why is that?' said Duke Ai.
Zhuangzi replied: 'One plus whatever

its source makes two, two and one
make three, and to balance them in light,
shadows and darkness, a fourth

emerges from them. Once four
arises, they criss-cross, and five appears
in their centre. Starting from nothing

to something, we reach five. And so it
goes on. Not even a skilled mathematician
can reach the end. Still, at the still

centre of the turning wheel, one
may still glimpse the infinite in all things.
Being keyhole to eternity, this point

is sole window on the inner history
of the universe, and of its neighbour,
nothing. But it is only a window.'

---

what's within   *accords with what's without*

5. Ways and Whys

'Then, everything is process, is
in process, changing to something else,
even stars,' said Duke Ai. But why?

Zhuangzi replied, 'Otters play and
chase each other under water. Gnats
dance in clouds over summer pools.

Geese and ducks migrate in V
formations. You and I dream and wake,
if we're lucky, 25,000 times. Then

we turn into bones nibbled by worms.
Stars explode and collapse. Others come.'
'I know,' said Duke Ai. 'But why?

It all strikes me as meaningless. What
is the reason for these absurd comings and
goings?' Zhuangzi said, 'All things

and creatures are Ways and Whys.
Non-life and life dance with each other.
Way turns to Why and Why to Way.'

using three chasers, losing the game   *to the fourth side, left open*

6. Things

'Why are things there
and here?' asked Duke Ai.
'What is their meaning,

their function? It's all
a puzzle to me. A huge
amazing maze. And

what am I doing here any-
way? I haven't a clue who I *am*.
Or even *is*.' Zhuangzi replied,

'The meaning of things
isn't separate from what
they really are –

from what they
actually, merely, simply, are.
Water-drop, tree,

fish, mountain,
emerald, speck of dust,
you, me – anything.'

(9)

Small Blessing, Possessing

---

wind   *over heaven*

On a slow train between Cambridge and King's Cross

Loopy summer. Our train
has stopped at Baldock and now
is off again. Curved wires be-

tween pylons. England's
greennesses hedge the line.
Ding dong. The next

station is Letchworth. Plat-
form hung with flower baskets.
Overhead lamps panelled

blue and white. Sky grey
and darker grey against grey.
Fields golding slow towards

harvest. Ding dong. The
next station is Hitchin. Field
banded by poppies and

silvering willows. To be
alive is good. To be alive and
well even better.

1. Green and red

Green, the open flimsy
curtains, and red, the frame
of the sash window

at the foot of our bed
where this afternoon I
lie, lazy, reading

and green, your tall
potted houseplant growing in
front of the window, and

green, the rowan
framed outside it
against the sky

and brilliant
red, the rowan's
berry clusters

a pair of thrushes
nonchalantly
peck and scatter.

---

it flares suddenly   *then dies down*

2. The nonplussed pleasures of love

Here I salute the implausible
and nonplussed pleasures
of love, the needed but

difficult kinship
even with invisible and
interior enemies, the far

simpler, easier sympathy with
the non-human, with creatures,
with the felt and observed

inanimate world, and their
embodiments and tracks –
and then to the sheer

facts of my breath, of you
and me improbably being
both here, together, alive. Is

Death the condition without
which such a life would be
unacceptable?

---

hand in hand   中道   *return to the central way*

3. Productions

Fanny the maid
enters. She screams.
The entire crew

suffers from
fits. Swine, blurts
the mutinous

scene shifter. Blast
your stubbled chin
on the trapeze.

You turn away.
I turn away. We
all turn away.

Canny whispers
pierce the palace's
refined spruces.

Till three o'clock
or whenever, calls the
Director. Be there.

spokes fall   *off the wheel, crash*

4. Night, curtains open

On the window's
dark outside, rain
pearls and runnels

and on its inside
the light accurately
reflects itself.

We can't see
outside, at least not
yet. But these

identities soon
will fray anyway
and what they

hold spill over in
whatever dark or light
surrounds them –

which is just as it
should be and cause for
neither grief nor joy.

---

then fancies fly away   *he'll fear not what men say*

5. Abbey Pool

Mid-January. Tuesday noon.
Two hours at Abbey Pool. Six
lengths plus spell in sauna.

Repeat five times. Stretch,
pull, breathe long. Lanes busy
with crawlers from Marshall's

in their lunch-break. I too
breast-stroke, back-stroke,
crawl. By half-past-one,

all lanes have emptied but
for pensioners. Mothers coo
to infants in paddling pool.

Shower cold then hot then
dress. Baby wails in nearby
changing-cubicle. Stroll

back to old grey Citroen.
Edging wind-laden car park
a willow begins greening.

6. Under rain

All summer rain
has been falling on
this thin flat roof –

brushing of cymbals
hammers drumming
gongs chiming –

as if wolves were
howling rocks clashing
forests tumbling –

and no blocking of
ears will keep out this
baying thrumming –

is this the onset
of the world's end
eve of judgement –

and in this heavy
sultriness will this
head crack open?

---

rain falls, stops, falls   *keep going*

Treading

a lake   *flooded by sky*

Water in the stone jug

Reflections off water
in the stone jug on our table
wander over walls

doodle across ceiling
because of noon breeze
and pool and still

above our fireplace.
Always light above and
light's inflections most

keenly inject glory
through tunnels in
tissues behind eyes.

With indelible marker
light injects and scores
photon-streams seared

through this, always
the one same unspellable
new-old name-of-names.

1. Spread white rushes

Spread white rushes
underneath, with a quiet joy
in the challenge, to be met

by measured caution –
hands washed and open,
breath clear, regular,

feet slightly apart, knees
and shoulders unstressed,
supple eyes prepared

to take in all angles,
ears filtering slightest
sounds – all of which

accumulate to a poised,
coiled, sustained alertness –
so treading on anything is

delicate as a small bird's
footprints on snow, a sturdy
bee's on stamens.

2. What the tinker said (1)

All earth is my
dwelling place,
said the tinker,

until this heart
stops. This road
ahead swirls

in and out of
rainbows. No way
could be clearer.

Under black light
earth remains pupil
in heaven's eye

and under sun
among blues, greens
and yellows, so

long as blood
flows in my veins
vision carries.

3. A shimmer of leaves

Whatever *I* was
or is or even seems
has vanished

into a shimmer
of leaves between
what and what

and what. What's left
for now is these graven
strokes on this park's

greeny floor, as
shadows of tree-trunks
and leaves sharpen

and fade, then fade
and sharpen. These
marks, this residue

constantly dissolving
and recrystallising, this
efflorescence.

4. Treading, gingerly

At blurred edges
of the possible, up against
the triple border between

what seems as yet
unknown, what rests ever
unknowable, and

this, inalienable –
gingerly he treads. Not an ant
is to be squashed by his

plodding heavy feet, nor
fruitfly be crushed by his
shaking clumsy hands.

Accident by negligence here
is not excusable. Weak links,
living treasures, are to be

nurtured in patience and
whatever is most fragile be
made strong. To live.

treading on a tiger's tail   *careful, careful*

5. In the desert (2)

And shall we tell you of
tented night? Having passed
droughts and sandstorms,

we with eyelids creased
who inhabit desert places
see shimmerings on our

purple velvet sky-bowl.
Beautiful? Yes, yet harder
far than the land we

tread, our dusks being
onset but never fulfilment,
for when our sun goes

kinging behind our skies,
Al-Qamar strolls out among
sequinned companions.

You who live among mists
and clouds know opalescent
fires. Our skies, diamond.

6. Poem for Daphne

Dear friend – I
wanted you to know
it has been a joy

to be alive here in
part of the same time-
space as you –

not just because of
things we've enjoyed
and shared but

because the gifts
you've given out-
paragon those

that goddesses and
gods are jealous of
in mortals – depth,

heroism in Death's
face, intellect, discernment,
spirit, magnanimity.

(11)

Harmonising, Prospering

---

earth rides exalting   *astride heaven*

In King's College Chapel

Today walking with Stefano
in King's College Chapel, as we
wander around Cambridge,

looking up, I find
myself counting. On each side,
twelve stained windows

and, above, where eyes
can't help ascending, fugues
vaulting. Each

fan's central line marks
one of twelve traves spanning
ceiling width. Echoing

from both sides of each stony
crossbeam, six doubled lines ring
gong-like through mind's

quiet, spilling and splaying
out glory apparent spreading
like peacock's tail feathers.

---

the petty has departed   *the great approaches*

88

1. Harvesting (1)

In harvesting a fertile
field, pulling out one firm
root may yield five more.

As seeds may breed to
feed multitudes, so in action
among men and women

calling on and calling out
one person in one generation
now may lead to many

more later, to wake, join,
prosper. This he understood,
one quiet man who later

became wartime leader,
then general, then minister,
then president, in an age

of peace and harmony
among people and peoples
that lasted centuries.

pull up a root   _others come away with it_

2. Embracing the waste land

Shang's ancestors were brave,
hardened warriors, men of another
world you won't find now.

They embraced the waste land
as if fighting a tiger with bare hands,
as if crossing a rocky river with

bare feet, as if knotting a snake's
neck after being poisoned by it, dying
without hint of regret or fear. Now

is time for this same primeval
struggle while deploying subtler arts –
magnanimous vision and patient

open heart, giving courage alike to
quick-witted sharp-eyed youngsters,
and uncouth rustic old-timers, by

marrying centre with periphery, far-
flung hamlets and frontier outposts
with provincial city and metropolis.

---

bonding by abiding   中道   *in the brilliance of the central path*

3. Constancy

Whatever was taken
away has gone for good.
Setbacks suffered now

invite inner strength
and courage. All roads
wind up and down

at some point
eventually. Though hope
creaks and falters

and prospects dim
and fade, to stay on
course at all costs

through good luck
and bad, coolly constant
to constancy, is what

matters, regardless of
fate's churnings, twists,
setbacks, backlashes.

one here will constant be   *come wind, come weather*

4. Among neighbours

Why flutter
palpitating heart, when
trouble trickles

panic through you?
Why trail blame on
its ashen way

when such moves
will winnow nothing
from nothing?

Sifting mind's
caverns is worth
more than ever

wish could bode.
A neighbour's trust
makes fuller sense

for wealth won't
win you more than
empty zeroes.

---

5. Working for Laban

He went out from the stony place
where he had dreamed of the ladder,
to Padan-Aran. And there he saw

Rachel, Laban's second daughter,
come down to water her father's flocks
at a stone-covered well. And he lifted

the stone, and kissed her. So she ran
to her father. And he said, Lord Laban,
Give Rachel to me in marriage and

I will work for you seven years. But
after his time of servitude had passed,
Rachel and her elder sister Leah

tricked him, preferring – deferring
to – the rights of the first-born. In
the bridal bed's curtained shadows

Leah took her sister's place. Laban
made Jacob work seven more years
before he could marry Rachel.

low above high   *blessing and fortune*

6. Past zenith

In brick cracks
grass grows. Weeds root
wanting wilderness.

Dust decks king's
castles. Trash carpets
cathedrals. Princes'

palaces crumble.
Decay drips down once
whitewashed walls.

Mould stains steps
and spiral stairways.
Gleaming water

wears away what
was glass and glaze.
Great halls fall.

Take heart. Time
to admit patterning
of inevitable fate.

walls fall   *back in the ditch*

(12)

Stagnating, Decaying

---

heaven split off   *from earth below*

Decay

Skies slept, or
looked the other way.
Exonerate nobody.

The eye of
heaven detached.
Justice cataracted.

On earth, men
slaughtered, fell
and rotted

and the dead
and living dead
sank deeper in decay.

Darkness flowered
in cruelty. Gracelessness
numbed hope.

Heaven there, world
here, and their only
meeting place, death.

1. Harvesting (2)

In fields on fire
one flame fuels five,
all of which seed,

breed, bleed, into
each other instantly,
constantly.

Fear too infects
people's skins and
hearts far faster

than fire. But so
do courage, hope,
loyalty. This he

knew in his guts,
his bones, one quiet
man who came

to call on, call out
cowed passive peasants
from indentured farms.

pull up a root   *others come away with it*

2. Collusion

Rottenness spread
so normally, so spiced
and glazed with reason

most believed it inevitable
and universal. Few noticed
this was no product of

'wild' nature, or natural
'law', but of cultivated
controlled operations

by profiteers and complicit
acolytes. Whether ensuing
corruption derived from

conscious conspiracy
among the ruling élite, whole-
sale communal collusion

or patterned itself on subtler
eruption of mass psychosis is
anybody's theory or guess.

3. The Charge

Never mind pasts
or backgrounds, all
were charged with

destiny. Many stayed
at home, tried
to go on working,

wore old habits,
maintained traditional
hope, sweated or

shivered for proper
reward in season,
followed paternal pattern

and parental prescription,
shuttered or buried minds
in custom and duty. Little

or nothing worked for
them. Who survived or died
was, they said, a lottery.

---

embrace shame   *bear it*

4. In the margins

Those who read the times
back into their grains
knew what to do

even though they knew
they didn't know enough
to know the whole game's

rules, let alone outcome,
and, trusting not hopes
but hunches and dim

premonitions, fled
cities and well-kept villages
and by lakes or marshes

or, higher up, on moorland,
erected makeshift shelters,
built huts, cleared caves,

trimmed and pared hope,
to train and prepare
for whatever might come.

5. Leader

After events, all
origins are obscure, and
so they seem now

of him who emerged
leader. Cometh the hour
cometh the man, say

historians, which
explains nothing of him
worth anything. 'He

honed himself to the time's
needs as to his people's, who
followed him. He shaped

them to his own and
made them a force, his own.
Opportunistic, cunning,

deep, indeed, but simple,
with scant gift for prophecy,
he read destiny's lines.'

for a windbreak   *forget not, pass not, perish not*

6. A sacrifice

What fact or factor
determines who'll be a hero
with the blind courage

to lead, by design
or impulse, and against
all odds of chance, who'll

be ready to follow him
and who'll, rather, stay at home,
be swallowed up by ruin,

victimise others, murder
by rote or proxy, flee into
exile, fatten and get rich,

mine chaos, exploit it –
and who'll go down giving
his own life, own death,

to save another, a stranger, like
Maksymilian Kolbe, Auschwitz,
1941, for Franz Gajowniczek.

with men like him   *how could things stand still for long*

(13)

Gathering, Togethering

fire   *under heaven*

To a next-door-neighbour

This tide of summer perfume
neither respects nor knows
any silly boundaries

of private property.
Look how the honeysuckle you
planted below our fence

has crept through cracks
and stretched, clutched, wound,
inflected and inflicted

its thousands of spiralling
tendrils around everything
it has encountered – all

apparently, to invade
my back garden in full-frontal
assault – from where its limbs

go on exploring in tangled
waves, tossing out flowers,
combing sweetnesses.

---

shared mind and heart   *action steel-sharp, words of jasmine*

1. Broken blur, crimsoned

A woman knocks at my
door. Light behind her unfolds.
It streaks through my

half-sleep. I don't want to
wake but do. I open my eyes
and am blinded. She is all

broken blur, crimsoned,
ripples on a lake. *This is
the one to whom you*

have been assigned. With
both forefingers I rub my eyes.
Thank you, I reply. And hear

my voice hollow, crusted –
as if not mine. But she is
still flickering, pellucid.

A blood-vessel in my
head bursts. A black sun
breaks like an egg.

2. Ventura Street

On the posh side
of Ventura Street, media
creatures, wannabees,

mediocrities, celebs
fix things up, splash
everywhere lies

conducive to their
own advancement. They
twang the networks.

Clinging together
woolly, they climb
the agencies,

promote one another
baa-baa-ing, supportive,
how original we are.

The top ones have
clambered over various
others' corpses.

together in a common clan   *degrading*

3. My neighbour my comrade

Now I shall be a good
deal more attentive to your
quiet voice and the work

you are still doing in
and for and around time
as you go walking

around my dream as
if you knew all the ways
through and out of it

and into and around
my house and my life
and I shall also be far

more appreciative of
your visits regardless
of how you choose

to arrive and disappear
my neighbour my comrade
my dear dead friend.

4. Good morning my dears

Good morning, my dears. Is that
you still standing outside, blocking
my rattling door? The dead

who call in the small hours
shortly before each dawn chorus
have a good deal more to say

than this limping man, this
boy with knife-slashed face, this
girl whose invisible bruises

still hurt and terrify her. Friends,
do you go the same way? I suspect
so in your eyes each time you

turn and look back – your bravery,
your bravura – comrades, companions,
strangers. All answers fall short,

people around here don't know
anything, suffering has no end.
What's the point of enemies?

---

mounting city walls, unable to attack   *so don't try*

5. Togethering

When our team got together,
we watched our own backs. We
complained to one another

about one another. We all
gossiped. We all denied we gossiped.
Our training? Tough.

First, they tested us in practice
on home terrain. Some couldn't
compete or complete. Fell out,

got sent home. Then no more
trials. Only combat, the real thing.
Now we know who our brothers

and sisters are. Our line is so
strong it can't be breached. Our
hearts and minds together

cut steel. Our mutual
words, though clipped, are
jasmine, honeysuckle.

first howling and wailing   *later, laughter*

6. Recluse

Why have you come to live in this
shack? To listen to wild geese, wind,
and swish and wash of waters

under this cloud-capped peak?
Commune with seasons, sparrows,
and hordes of croaking toads?

Live off berries, fishes, and milk
from two lean goats? Commendable,
to quell mind, calm spirit, here,

but who is there to talk to?
Battles to be fought and friendships
to be won must be taken on

with people, in the city. Your
task is only half-done and you need
to return now. Unless of course

I'm mistaken and you aren't
the one I've been sent to find
to guide and lead our army.

---

harmonising with nature   *task incomplete*

(14)

Huge Having

---

fire   *over heaven*

111

Order in grand design

Fundamental axiom under-
lying all tropes and genres
in all literary arts, as in

all singing, all music,
all mathematics, all science,
is the sense of and desire

for order, not only already
within, but discoverable and
not imposed: coherence

of all separable discrete
entities in a grand design,
the ways they all fit,

how fitting it all is, how
suitable, at all levels, from
the most tractable forms

threaded on the known and
probable to apparently least
significant hidden strings.

1. Out walking

Early I stand against my
familiar beech tree and look
up past its mossed silvery

bark through shimmering
interplays of light and leaves.
Tree, you have called me

time and again out walking
to stand under you and know
hushed heaven-inklings. For

that, whatever-I-or-me-is
loves you. Am the only one
so far out walking today.

Hollyhock heads quiver
under strengthening wind
across gardens. Ginger

tom pauses in allotment
under sunflower. Young
blackbird watches.

no pride, only calm   *no damage, no harm*

2. Ground

Slice mind into two
modalities, sleeping and
waking, and of each

make six further cuts, or
more. Putting them back
together in language

repatterns human spirit
and engenders poetry as
hope, as act, as ground-

base of firmed world
in a fineness so very fine
no perfume could so

much as hint at its
fullness. Here poetry
as foundation

also of states and
processes of being is
equally affirmed.

a big wagon   *for loading*

3. Thanks and praise to my beech tree

Called when out walking
spellbound, to enter your protective
tent, your bough-ring of leaves,

time and again I've been pulled
through harsh times' despairings
to rest and lean, palms

splayed behind me a-
gainst your silver bark, fingers
pressed into your cool

life, tuned and resonant
to your patient power. And
against hope I'd maintain

hope of drawing down sky's
influences through you, to allay
terrors and keep those I love

from harm. Today, seeing
several such outcomes delivered,
thanks I bring and praise.

4. An old man on the beach

A man aged seventy-seven
sits on a beach playing with
pebbles. He did the same

aged seven. Now
he entrains his breath to rise
and fall flush with the hiss

and whish of the long
slow-lapping tide. His eyes
are closed and his mind

opens, expands, half-
empties. He has walked down
here to the sea from a

house on the shore-road
and his legs are sturdy as
he stands and stretches.

His pulse beats steady
as his open eyes take in
the generous horizon.

5. Dark gates of things

Sometimes dark
gates of things do open
and at their edges

gaps get left
by meanings comp-
letely falling away

and borders and edges
between and among things
that once were claimed

definite, defined –
though being even more
markedly present than

might have appeared
before – nevertheless
now simultaneously

flow into one
another, merge,
blend, bond.

the fortune of her dignity   *shines through*

6. Shadowless beings

Shadowless beings
from the mind's caves
haunt him in sleep.

Are these the kind
ones who will escort
whatever remains

of him at life-end
to dissolve in peace
and nothingness?

They rise out of mist,
these, the lightbearers,
but have no part in it.

Among all other fig-
ures of dreams, these
call rarely.

They say nothing.
Made of light itself,
they smile.

(15)

Humbling

---

under earth   *a mountain*

Way

What is low
sits on what is
most high

having little
hoarding nothing
wanting nothing

willing nothing
winning nothing
nothing wanting.

What is, it
shares, splits
and spills

brags not
complains not
bullies not

divides
without despair
dispassionate.

---

1. Getting down in

The gate was shut against
us so we retrenched among
high limestone boulders

hidden behind the lodge.
Flaky but full of crannies for
footholds and handholds

these we scaled with ropes
and slings but no hammer
or hint of clink by metal.

Then a shorter climb down
to the lodge roof and through
it by loosening slates, into

what we now believe the
central cavern, from where
this report is sent. By

torchlight many grooved
rhomboid forms appear carved
in ornate panels on the walls.

slow, quiet   *the large, careful work*

2. We wash things

We wash things, pour
oil on them, use them
for carrying, cooking,

cutting. Meanings
slip from one thing to
another. Things also

take wing through
time, acquiring and
discarding meanings

like feathers. It's
small particles model
and mould dooms.

Yet spaces between
will open and ways names
blur one another be

cleared. But who is it
will do the opening and
renaming, and return?

3. She sweeps shadows

She sweeps shadows
from oblong flagstones,
diamond tiled walls

and mosaic-planked
floors. Careful
to spill no single

speck, she collects
shadow-dusts
in an angled pan

whose contents
she tips in
a black silk bag

tied with plaited
flame-coloured
strings. Each

evening she does this
and spills the bag
across night.

4. Apprentices

Why should you complain,
Maître, when your students,
trainees, apprentices –

those you've selected,
encouraged, promoted from
ranks, nurtured for

their talents, and taught
everything you know – turn
away and supersede,

ignore, pass over, even
despise you? Whether they
surpass you or not,

their part-function is
to humble you. So be
thankful. And make

way for this your
second apprenticeship
in modesties.

5. Old washerwoman

Old washerwoman came
to Gautama. 'Teach me to meditate,'
she said. 'There's no sitting still

in my life. I'm on my feet from
before dawn till long after dusk.
I work knee-deep in water.

Feel the river flowing around
and inside me. I've never known
stillness. I'm so tired each night

I sleep as soon as my head hits
my bunk. And I dream of the river
washing me away. I know

that's how my death will come.
Tell me, Lord, how can I find time
to start to learn to meditate?'

'Mother,' Gautama smiled,
'I thank you. You have just
taught me how to meditate.'

6. When hope ended

When hope ended
she prayed, for modesty
above all. Then she put

her modesty back below
in the lowest of all possible
places she could imagine,

lower than graves
where corpses rot, lower
than tunnelling trains,

lower than sewers
under cities, than rats
that slink along them,

than coalmines, than
oceans, than sticky oils
locked beneath them,

lower than any hells
she might have incurred
or be about to suffer.

(16)

Delighting

---

thunder   *over earth*

Somewhere to go

It furthers one to have
somewhere to go. The further
from home the better. Get

out and about, see nature in
all her glory, meet lots of people,
talk, find out their stories,

have amazing adventures. In
the future, all futures, everything
is possible, as all children who

can and may hope, know –
hope being the condition of children
so long as it hasn't been smashed

or tortured out of them. So
go, spend a life finding out what
it is you have to find. Travelling

itself being perfection, all jour-
neys are endlessly homebound and
every departure is homewards.

1. Stargate One is open

Stargate One is open. You
are required to go through it
and vanish. However slick

and polished responses
or lack of them, go anyway.
You may be too early for

encouragement. Grasp, grip,
then let go. We have conned all
the old charts, scoured and

scried all likely locations.
Slender the chances, outrageous
the odds against. Therefore

grow in, grow down
gloryless. Necessary modesty
won't reward you as you had

hoped but may otherwise
surprise. The key, transparency,
your own breathing.

singing out, delight   *it will end*

2. Go here

Go here Here
HERE, called the bird
repeatedly in

many forms
and guises. The small girl
on the path

did just that. She
hopped, skipped and leaped
and then stopped to

get her breath
back. And laugh. She laughed
and laughed. Leaves

above her swayed in
greeny agreement. Below her
a river tinkled arguments

in ceaseless bells. Her
eyes saw the sun doubly
then singly reflected.

3. Sleep's club is closed

At the end of Rope All-
ey the sign says Singles Bar
in green and red neon

but sleep's club is clo-
sed to you in particular
clutched in cramps.

The tortured stomach
knots and the spine
burns in silence.

The blood on its buck-
ing roundabout throws off
its riders and passengers.

Twist rattle knock push
as you will – nothing will do
any good. The bouncer will

throw you back thudding
on the walkway your heart
must pound until dawn.

delight, wallowing   *regret*

4. *Beli andjeo*

Beli andjeo appeared,
human-sized, long-haired
wings tipped blue, gold.

I knew him an angel
since he breathed airlessly
smiled without seeming

saw without looking
heard without my speaking
and understood the

split instant my own
thought formulated. So
in my mind I asked –

What must I do now?
Follow, the angel replied,
Follow the book's path –

winds to danger's core
words to the dragons' cave
hopes to the tiger's lair.

gather allies as the hair-clasp   *gathers hair*

5. She wrote herself into Death

Gillian Rose wrote
herself into Death. When
Death came for her

Gillian was writing. She
looked at Death head on
and through her words

confronted Death in
writing. So she met Death
at the end of words,

her words, their end.
And although Death stared
Gillian out, and like a rose

she shrivelled, withered,
rotted into dust, into ash –
into nothing – it is not

nothing Gillian did by
rising to write right into
Death's invisible face.

6. Lovers

Between their noses
not quite touching, an
hourglass made of air

a leaf hanging
on time and time
hung on a leaf

Between their smiling
eyes and mouths, a vase
of transparent nothing

they drank water
from rocky places un-
filtered still by herbs

Between this face
of now and that, they
burned down dawn

interlocked bodies
swept entire starry
nights of dust

---

dark delight reaches the top   *how could it last long*

(17)

Following

Rules

Rules that govern
the gatherings of rooks
into creaking colonies,

V formations of geese,
vastnesses of herring shoals,
bees' mouth-shapes

to fit particular flowers,
also govern patterns of
your mortal time

to its destiny and
your destiny through time.
Now therefore is when

to submit your
habitually warring
and undisciplined

spirit in willing
modesty to what
needs be done.

1. Old dog

When I look in your eyes
old dog, I wonder if you're
following me or I you. As

I stroke your old head,
admiring as ever the cool sleek
tuning of your body, of your

entire being, I wonder too
if you're thinking, and if so,
what, of what. Years ago

I trained you, to work,
do my bidding. I followed
your unerring senses, trim

speed-bursts, ever clear
judgement, as you followed
your nose. Now you're

going blind, it's me
works for you, old dog. But
still I'm following you.

situation changed   *keeping steady*

2. Other voices

I bear strong
kinship with these other
voices, not mine,

that speak inside my
head and heart and here
more truly than any

I might ever call
my own. These voices
that have no

mouth except in
your mouth, no breath
but in your own

lungs' breathing, tell
me where to go, what
to do, and how.

I follow straight
without complaint
or grief.

3. A thing like this

Making a thing like this means
following twin perspectives, as in
building a mosaic. While along

one you follow each parcelled
fragment, its unique resonances
to light and touch, the other

you let wander over the whole
design, its soarings and cascades,
fractal novelties and intricate

repetitions, which turn
and tune space to music. And
when details and the whole

correlate and intertwine,
when patterns take care of one
another (and of you), they

let you let go of all old skills
and all old selves. Whatever you
were falls away, irrelevant.

following first small things   *then the large*

4. Aamil al Ahmad

Aamil al Ahmad lined walls,
paved floors and coated inner
and outer domes in minuscule

squares of pasted stone. Jade,
mother-of-pearl and glazed clays
he deployed. Limestone, granite

and marble he cut. Glass he
smelted to perfection, massing
fragments in infinite shades

and nuances to pattern
heaven's pleats unfolding through-
out multi-layered creation.

His views on articulating the
Unnameable, his critics claimed
heretical. Yet the Sultan so

adored his subtle geometries
and delicate tessellations, no de-
tractor could ever touch him.

---

the strong following the strong   *keep heads low*

5. You

The book is constantly
being written. Made though
it may be (*will be, has been*),

always there's a fault in it,
some minor imperfection,
fissure, sliver, gap, crack –

into and through which
you enter, whoever you may be.
Following, you fill, you fulfil

the book. You straddle it,
leap into it and complete it.
Singular, unique *you*,

final piece in its puzzle,
end-cog, wired connection
completing its circuit,

switching it on, off, on,
you open and close the book
with no back cover.

6. Across hill country

Rebels proclaimed rule across
hill country as far as our western
border. We sent in an army.

Villagers in valleys didn't want
war anyway, didn't care who ruled,
so long as they got fair treatment.

We starved rebel strongholds
out till only stragglers were left,
pariahs half-starved in caves

feeding off rats and berries.
We stripped their leader of
weapons, boots, armour,

led him off bareheaded,
bound behind a nag. Later
the king himself climbed

our westernmost mountain
where he sacrificed an ox to
mark our border again.

(18)

Rotting, Remedying

A thickening of adversities

He digs for edible roots
from bracken beds beneath
rotting oaks among

last year's acorns. What
he has to drink in this land,
he says, is disillusion, and

to taste, his own bile. What
he will wield is a dagger, now
sheathed against his shin,

bullet-belt digging into
shoulder, rifle and bayonet
ready. The path he'll

tread is as yet unmade.
It winds through forests and
crosses mountains. Others

will join him there. What
little he traces before him is
a thickening of adversities.

1. Clearing, replanting

Could the task be managed?
What we needed, claimed Chiara,
was a *plan*, teamwork, effort,

plus reams and reams of patience.
Evacuate the whole area. Relodge
survivors. Rebuild strengths,

health, confidence, willpower.
Provide meals, medicine, teachers
for young and able, care for old

and weak. Long term: create
jobs. Appoint experts. Bring in
equipment and instruments.

Test foundations. Redesign
structures. Tear down whatever
wasn't fit for service or futures

and rebuild. With local teams
in control, making all decisions.
Plant saplings, shrubs, bushes.

2. Beaten

Marta caved in under
beatings, blackmail and
financial double-binds.

Body and hands being
her only dowry, how could
she have been more

than chattel, indentured
to him in perpetuity? How
could her rewards for

multiform variable tasks
not have been dependent
on his whim and dictate?

Once he had emptied
a bottle's contents down his
gullet, he turned bully.

Now he's dead, how can
and why should she, broken
and battered, mourn?

3. An apprentice

Brisk, confident, but blind
in assumptions and certainty,
Jo screws up nearly every

time she moves. She can't
not do this, knotting simplest
tasks into errors, howlers,

horrors. Whether she'll
learn or unlearn from past
impetuosities or go

on bumbling, fumbling,
stumbling over whatever
she gets anywhere near

let alone lays a finger on
remains to be seen. Though
she's all tacky thumbs she

believes and insists only
she knows right. She might
get it if only she'd listen.

eager, getting   *it wrong*

4. Old rot

Called in to clean things up,
with minimal training and no
experience, Malcolm needed

practical advice, help, drive.
So who else should he call on
but old reputed experts? Yet

Malcolm didn't register
how indelibly and ineradicably
were inscribed their interests

in models and infrastructures
of obsolete systems. To cure
decay, its unscanned causes

not its symptoms needed up-
rooting. Malcolm's policies, built
on fudges, makeovers, and

whitewashes, with ancient per-
sonnel sporting new names and
titles, perpetuated old rot.

ineffectual reform   *repeats humiliation*

5. Clearing up

Confident and fair-minded,
son of an intelligent father, young
Suleyman's tasks at outset were

hardened by cabals and cliques
sponsored by ambassadors of
several neighbouring states

avid to take advantage – and
possibly invade and colonise –
plus influential home-based

industrialists and financiers
restless and ambitious for shrewd
self-advancement. Aware of

his vulnerabilities, Suleyman
possessed far more than adequate
supplies of his father's astuteness,

and appointed administrators
who, against all pressures, oozed
loyalty, authority, confidence.

---

inheriting, establishing   *confidence*

6. Recluse, autumn morning

Looks up at mountain,
purple, pink, blue. Clouds
climb, cloak his peak,

cluster to cover it.
Patched early sun perches,
wrinkles pine tops.

Wind twirls, drums on
cones' scales and needles,
brushes dew-showers.

Looks down at old hands,
finger-fans, knuckle-knobbles,
veins vaulted, tunnelled rivers.

To hear the here, know
the now, know the here, hear
the now – *all one*. Inner

and outer funnel each
other. Before first snows,
he basks in this.

---

he who once served kings   *now studies the now*

(19)

Approaching

---

earth   *over lake*

Young Arthur

Feet planted on
clouded hills, heels
rooted in centuries,

calves and thighs hide-
covered, hips and groin
sheathed in bearskin,

heart healed by living
waters, eyes and ears
sky-filled, star-rooted,

head thonged in owl's
and blackbird's songs,
hands clenched tight

over one another,
close-clutching all
futures, in silence

a long-legged boy
approaches, heaves
sword from stone.

---

approaching sublime prosperity   *in the end dolorous*

1. Wind across grass

You can't watch wind, only
wind's effects. But can you see
how, here, across grass, time

may flow backwards too, as
floods of *was* and *will-be* inter-
penetrate, the unpredictable

unlikely casual tomorrow
and the firm and sure causal
arrow being mere surfaces

of the immense, patterned
dense-packed, multilayered
field you float in, through

and on? And then how
that whole field, with every
blade bobbing and falling

upon it, stops – an utterly
stilled pool no hint of breath
of breeze grazes or glazes?

---

approaching   *steadfast*

2. Sea Cave

Through this sea cave at all
times whistles wind. At low tide
for a few hours you can walk

from grassy clifftop down
winding crab-angled ledges
carved jagged in sea-face

and then a briny balancing
as, hand-over-hand, clambering,
clinging to boulders, before

you're aware of it, you find
you've already entered a vast
asymmetrical dome

where floor-molluscs keep
mouths tight out-of-water
and from roof-ledges cries

of thousands of nesting
birds magnify hollow echoes
eerily against sea thrum.

3. Into Coleridge Park

Today again I walk out
into Coleridge Park and
stand under my favourite

beech tree and press
my hands against its bark
and wish for peace. How

stupid and unnecessary
wars are when death will
get us all anyway. I write

this, my friend, to you in
a capital city under siege,
from a municipal park in

a provincial English town
where wind hums gusting
through leaves of every

tree under this island's
summer sky patched with
clouds and bluenesses.

4. Light encased in unhappened time

Light encased
in unhappened time,
unopened in eyes

of creatures unborn,
unformed yet as water
drops on pane

of sloping wind-
ow in unbuilt roof –
ungathered

in cistern or well,
and uncapped on
parched tongue

on any space-
crafted worldship –
playing here

among shadows
sudden in this
now total.

5. The end of Arthur

And when Sir Bedivere had
thrown the sword in the lake, an
arm and hand rose up straight

from the waters and grasped it.
So Bedivere carried Arthur down
from the chapel where he lay

wounded, to the waterside, and
a little boat hove in to the bank
carrying many beautiful ladies

to take him to Avalon, to heal
him of his grievous wound. Then
Sir Bedivere wept, for Arthur's

time had come. Arthur asked
the knight to pray for his soul,
and the boat slid away on

the waters out of Bedivere's
sight. Weeping and wailing, he
took himself into the forest.

approaching wisely　　　　　　　　*as is fit for a great king*

6. At Dragon Gate

Strokes of meteors
across mid-August midnight
signalled him quietness.

Moon expanded,
contracted and re-expanded
to fill his closed eyes.

Air currents swept
pollen-scents on salt-
laden sea-breeze.

He opened his eyes,
licked lips. Star-high his
body floated, lifted

and left by gravities.
He steadied vision, built
protective rings and

passed mind-ghosts
and monsters. This was
a man of our time.

(20)

Watching

---

wind blows   *over earth*

What the book said about itself

In opening this book
you open a locked chamber
in which, before words,

you have to read lines
to unlock the meanings
hidden in its words.

Meanings lie neither
in words nor in lines but
cluster behind both. Nor

will these leap to greet you
like puppies wagging tails
to welcome Master home.

You have to sit and wait
in a patience within patience
without praise or hope

for meanings to grow
like ferns unscrolling from
cracks between lines.

1. Patterns of our own

Stars' shifting positions,
forms of sunrise and sunset,
changes in moon-shape,

gradual wind-markings
on disappearing clouds, their
whorls, twists, edges, blurs,

mountain-shapes in mist,
textures of fur, skin and hair,
light's striations on water,

tracks made by animals,
birds, spiders, insects, worms
in sand, dust, mud, clay –

observing these high
and low with eyes peeled
we learned to copy

and with fingers mark
patterns of our own in shell,
wood, clay, hide, stone.

2. First came number

First came number
out of both nature and
our own minds – 'for

counting is in its
very essence magical, if
any human practice at

all is. For numbers
are things no one has
ever seen, heard or

touched. Yet they exist,
and their existence can be
confirmed in everyday

humdrum terms.
Numbers are instantly
available for every

counting operation,
like spirits that can be
conjured up at will.'

3. Changing into beautiful

What the book says of itself
is that first of all came numbers
taking forms of straight lines

like fingers, which gradually
folded in upon themselves
being and denoting

pattern in inner and
outer worlds, i.e. pattern
in pattern in pattern. As

zeroes marked higher orders
and orders within orders, one
plus zero equalled not one

but ten, and so on. So, like
beasts, fish and fowl, numbers
multiplied, breeding of

their own accord, changing
into more and more beautiful
forms, more subtle characters.

4. Numbers exist but do not

Numbers exist but do not,
being inherent in and among all
observable things and equally

so in all orderings and
patternings of our own inner
world. Out of one, two. Two

and one make three. In their
centre a fourth. And so it goes on.
'So natural number remains

the common ordering factor
of both physical and psychic
manifestations of energy.

Number draws psyche and
matter together. When energy is
manifest in either psychic or

physical dimensions, it is
always numerically structured,
as waves or psychic rhythm.'

5. Way Why One

In the beginning was
Word – and Word was
wholly *way why one.*

Word was number
and unison. Word was
one and all. And

Word was not spoken
but heard. In silence. Then
Speech copied Word.

Word did not copy
Speech. So Word bred,
numbering all things,

and itself proliferated.
In silence words married
words and marked

and mapped meanings.
So now in silence Word
reads, is read, in words.

6. Lines unbroken and broken

So we copied, counted
and measured, from what
we saw and heard –

eggs, shards, shells,
seeds, casings, stones,
cones, bones, entrails,

tails, scales, wings,
leaves, flowers, stems,
feathers, nails, bark,

thunder, waves, winds,
roots, shoots, shadows –
and so learned forms

and figures. So too we
carved necessity and made
patterns of our own

and from their cracks
and fissures drew lines
unbroken and broken.

(21)

Biting through

---

thunder   *under heaven*

Lean and strong

Lean and strong
poems, is how I want
you now, the way

you have to be. There's
nothing else for it. You
have to stand up

against Death and
in the face of Death
not collapse.

You have told me,
Throw away your
craft, your tricks,

your techniques, all
you have learned. I am
following your directions

so when Death blows or
calls me or anyone out, you
will pass, last, endure.

1. Across the bare langscape

In frozen word-skins
did Sydney Graham set out
across wastes for what else

was there worth doing in
a British poetic psychospace
occupied and monopolised

by liars, cheats, poltroons,
time-servers, time-wasters,
lickspittles, xenophobes,

sycophants, soulmongers,
and narcissists? Better go
out alone across the bare

langscape, taking nothing
for granted with no props but
his husky word-sentinels

themselves to pull and
track him and the wildernesses
between their howls.

2. In his wake

Though he has gone over
that no-talking-back horizon
and will never answer

my call I hereby
set out awake in
his wake even

though varying
direction. No other way
through or out of now

other than *this* now,
this knowing, this *nowing*
for poems. Yes being

and talking with you
all my lovely living friends
and family in blood and

flesh on webcam or phone
is fine fine. But poems call
now across our deaths.

3. Blandscape

Across this terrain, that might
have been called a *blandscape* had
it not been so inhospitable

in its dreary flatness, and were
its mottled skies not so huge and
varied – on foot and horseback

never stopping long, we
passed westwards, skirting
forest edges, guarding

ourselves and our animals
from direct blasting by winds,
keeping whenever we could

to firm ground, along ridges
bordering rivers, never too far
from water for our caravans.

Owls screamed around us
nights long. Dawn choruses
woke us. We kept moving.

4. Blackscape, Bleakscape

Then *Blackscape*, we called
it, and *Bleakscape*. All winter
snowdrifts piled high under

whirling gales. Summers
sank them in sodden swamps
gnat- and mosquito-infested,

cursed by every kind of
crawling thing. Yet winding be-
tween dangers, paths we wore

down opened into graziers'
routes. And in those slow times
between migrations of tribes

following us westwards, claiming
us kinsfolk, we drained and divided
fields, dug lodes and ditches

and learned to cut peat. Smoke
rose from our huts tucked among
stone-cleared strips and patches.

5. Through this inked silhouette

So into (the) language itself goes
this too, howling wolf-like against
falling silent snow – there

being no other presence out
there except yours on (the) other
side of this, whoever (ghost)

you may be (become) now.
By *that* time may you have taken
on flesh and sentience and

even speak, indeed, speak in
these words – until which time
must *this* lie muffled, stifled,

bound safe under thick
page-snow, beneath my breath,
frost in my throat – to be

heard (if it be called hearing)
only by your trawling, scrying
through this inked silhouette.

biting through   *dried meat, then clear*

6. Proud

We are those who crossed once,
twice, repeatedly. Many rivers we
forded and named. Days' heat,

evenings' flies, rats, spiders,
venomous snakes, we countered
and (mostly) controlled. Famine,

drought, flood, fire's ravages
despite losses, we endured and
survived. Plagues we witnessed,

somehow pulled through, and
many tribes fought and persevered
against, just as we battled inner

serpents, nightmare's contenders,
old hooded ones. Though battered,
we upheld honour; and though

punished, remained righteous. So
disdain to answer those who claim
us too proud for our own good.

right intention, wrong way   *deafened, punished*

(22)

Grace Adorning

fire   *beneath the mountain*

Under hills

Under hills, quiet
fire. From their graves
the dead awaken.

Blessing on you
who live, they call
through our own voices,

as in their places
we too shall call
our own unborn.

Under hills, this
grace flows
through everything.

Chestnut and oak
bud, green
earth's carpet.

Red tulip petals
scatter. A blue
butterfly hovers.

1. Leaf. Leaf.

Everything about this
perfect shining moment
hazes, fuzzes, furzes

into *un*, the way grasped
or ungrasped perfection always
shimmers at its edges

into something soluble,
not itself, different from,
other than, opposite to

everything it is, could be,
stands for. And that blur
keeps moving around

not just tomorrow or under,
forward, before, back, etc. Every
locative-temporal placement

of it falters, flickers, yes, *and*
internally, at core – that is, if it
has one. *Leaf. Leaf.*

---

2. Coolly calling

The rowan outside
our house had a pair of
ring-collared doves

sitting in its
summer foliage. You
whispered me up-

stairs to see. Earlier
in the summer, a green
woodpecker pitted

the trunk with
its beak. Now ripened
red berries are

dropping, it's the
turn of the blackbirds,
to preen and gorge.

Thank you for
coolly calling me
up here to see.

grace adorning   *tree branches*

3. Concerning light and her

She knows light
has the lightest touch
that sears and burns,

and light a kind
of *form* that reaches
around corners.

So light addresses
and dresses her, and
arrests false gazes.

She gathers light
in her arms and on
her shoulders, in

her belly and
breasts, and over her
forehead and eyes.

Wrists, knuckles,
thumbs and fingers
of light entwine her.

grace   *adorning, moistening*

4. When she sang in the bazaar

When she sang
in the bazaar, when she
uncurled her voice

a paid murderer swilling
coffee burned his lips
but did not curse

seven sparrows glancing
adoringly at airwaves
stayed put on their wire

five doped-out slaves
passing in chains lifted
stooped eyes, comprehending

the novice prayermaster
turned his head, his mouth
an awed O

and canny winds stopped
swirling, and blew seawards
orchestrally.

grace in white   *like a winged horse*

5. Now

Whenever you come
it is always now,
matterless, beginningless

and without warning
and the present is so
full of your presence

nobody notices what
you wear is your
own nakedness,

full to the brim
of your self only –
like a Chinese

paper lantern
containing fire,
moulding fire

in pastels, congruences,
self-consuming in
your own fire.

6. When she sang in the white alley

When she sang
in the white alley beside
the covered fruit market

the cheesemakers
and yoghurt pourers sighed
in their large blouses

a legless beggar, perched
on cardboard in his colonnade
stopped twitching his lips

for five long seconds
the corner butcher held
his cleaver in mid swipe

a ringletted redhead's irises
from their habitual brown
burned gold streaked green

and the woman selling
strawberries laughed
remembering something.

(23)

Peeling

mountain   covering earth

Concerning archaeology

A cat's jaw poked
up from the reed bed, slimed
with mildew and moss.

On the old battlefield
I found half a button, and
she, a pottery fragment.

Josh's fossil turned out
a nautiloid, black limestone,
400 million years old.

Air in these lungs
is thick with crumbled
shit dust. Meanings

that moan in dross
and memorabilia demand
magnified attention. We

traverse the field in
more and slower detail
to get anywhere at all.

rottenness   reaches the bed's legs

1. 'We thank our Führer'

'March 1938: the most popular sport that
weekend was to round up all ranks of Jews
particularly middle class specimens

and make them clean streets
and scrub pavements decorated with pro-
Schuschnigg posters and slogans

and kick and beat them especially
older and feebler ones if they stumbled
or collapsed. The Jews were forced

to work with bare hands onto which
acid was poured. Meanwhile Viennese
citizens stood by jeering and laughing

and occasionally breaking into roars
of delight as they chanted: "Work for the
Jews at last! At last work for the Jews!

We thank our Führer for finding
work for the Jews. We thank our dear
Führer for finding work for the Jews."'

2. The forensic archaeologist's testimony

In the area of Nyamata Church
atrocity was so widespread and
gang-rape so systematically

organised that men with
HIV waited their turn till last.
In a vault below that church

a particularly large coffin
was found, at least three
metres long. The body

inside was a woman's
of merely average height. She
needed this long coffin

because she had been raped
with a sapling. The tree had been
forced right through her.

The local people
buried her with the
tree inside her.

---

erosion, quake   *calamity, collapse*

3. After the massacre

Mouth of a dead shoe
squeaks toothless out of clay.
No those aren't vultures

they're jays, said
the Chairman. Be careful
with that spade.

Both local magnolias
and jacarandas have
been burned here.

Permaplastoid froth
covers and seals the
pools. A silver chain

surrounded several
joined vertebrae, reported the
bespectacled young forensic

archaeologist, wearing
a blue *hamsah* medallion
around her slender throat.

4. Language Palazzo

The Language Palazzo
caved in. Meanings
collapsed to rubble.

In the Hall of Great
Welcomes, monuments
crashed and splintered.

A precious library
housed on the *piano nobile*
tumbled into vaults.

Muddy canal waters
gushed in upon it
upsetting the lagoon.

Doom-laden analysts
loved it: *sluices not and
could vents replaced be.*

In the Campo de la Bragola
two children went on playing
blue-chalked hopscotch.

5. The prime-minister heliports

The prime-minister
heliports to an army
base seven

safe kilometres from
the refugee camp and
gets driven there in

an armour-plated jeep.
Cameras zoom into his
sincere sombre sober

warm composed face
as he sweats in rolled
up shirtsleeves inside

a tent, holding a two
year-old child on his
lap. It was worth it,

he says afterwards in
private, grinning, his
steely eyes glinting.

6. (A) coherent language

Enough of battering, blasting,
storming, excavating, carving.
Our job is to foster and grow

(a) coherent language, little
by little, in patience, in respect.
And how can this be but

by following the heart's
paths and injunctions – to
reaffirm the dignity

of the dead, and reclaim,
recall, rediscover – or find for
the first time (a) language

fit for, capable of examining,
expressing, understanding, *in*
and *through* words, what had

been unsaid, unsayable, and
so mend and change the real,
regrow and rebuild hope.

(24)

Returning

---

thunder   *under the earth*

Everyone knows the ways

Everyone knows the ways
home, across the valleys, where
the children are. Everyone sees

and recognises the trees
and gardens, the long avenues,
shapes of parks and pools.

Everyone knows at least
some of the ways after birth and
before death, and it isn't hard

to read maps and apply them.
But who except voices like these
will take you and me on

into zones the other silent
and unwritten side before
birth and after death, where

light itself gleams brilliant
black and angelic against
interiors of mountains?

1. Home east

They went or came home
east, from the same country into
the same country they had

escaped or been exiled
from, back to places and spaces
memory-distilled from childhood

where, as in a haphazardly
sequenced dreamlike timewarp,
they found everything as if

nothing had changed at all.
Then, re-returning west to the
'new' places they had chosen,

or, rather, had been chosen
by – when they told their stories
to their now suddenly other and

unfamiliar companions, long-
locked tears streamed down
their shocked reawakened faces.

beautiful   *return*

2. Both ways meant exile

They said they had spoken dialects
they hadn't heard aloud in years,
got drunk with uncles and

unfamiliar grown-up cousins who
still lived like their grandparents.
Their journey in space had seemed

as if back through time, and
they had shivered, laughed, wept,
taken photos of recognised

courtyards, houses, streetlamps,
trees that had blossomed in childhood,
and then returned west to their better

paid jobs, friends, partners. But
going or coming both ways, they said,
now meant double exile. To inhabit

either zone incurred loss of the other,
home being in neither. Differences
blurred between forward and back.

3. With her own old key

Without error, with-
out terror, with her own
old key which, oddly,

still fitted the lock
at 4 a.m. she quietly
let herself back in

the house she had left,
the house she had been
forced out of. She freed

back blinds, threw open
windows and shutters and
sat waiting for dawn slowly

to wake its occupiers. She
no longer wanted or expected
revenge or recompense.

It was just for the chance
to see and read their eyes
when they recognised her.

returning again   *and again*

4. Emigrant's daughter

An emigrant's daughter
from another land and language
travelled years later 'back' to

the nightmare place forbidden
by her own tribe's enemies – she
who when they had conquered,

had she then been born, would
have been to them as slime,
poison, vermin. Although now

most prized and praised, and
even adored and darlinged by
her cultured, earnest lover, a

son of the tribe of her parents'
enemies – wherever she walks
in his powerful city, she keeps

stumbling upon herself,
nudging and hugging shadows,
huddled, stooping, wary.

5. Under the bridge

The Rabbi of Krakow dreams.
Under a big bridge in Łodz lies
a treasure. He leaves, disguised

as a beggar. After many days'
walking, he finds his dream-bridge.
A Cossack is guarding it.

'Officer,' he says, 'I heard
a treasure is buried here, right
under this bridge. Is it true?'

Cossack guffaws. 'Ignorant
beggarman, why, last night I had
a dream. Some old fool rabbi

travelled here from Łodz.
He'd had a dream of a treasure
under this bridge. He could

have saved his legs. It is
buried in his own hearth.' Rabbi
bows thanks. Goes home.

6. I know a house

I know a house that has
so many rooms you could
never explore them all.

Door gives on corridor,
corridor on door, door on
chamber, and chamber

on interior garden. Every
time you go back, between
blinks, asleep or awake –

despite appearances, shared
views from numberless windows,
dusty and irregular panes,

paucities of wish and
limits of desire – no room is
a copy of any other, nor

even similar. And from this
side, you can open all doors.
But from the other, none.

(25)

Untwisting

thunder rolls   *under heaven*

Only breathe in corners

'Only breathe in corners and
when you touch the winds, I mean
walls,' said the girl. 'When

you're in the middle you're not
allowed to breathe in at all – only
out. Look, like this.' And she

stood in the corner and sucked
air in with huge breath and voice
creaking. Then with hands

stretched out either side she
waved them up and down faster
and faster until she zoomed

into the room's centre where
she hovered for 19.43 seconds
wholly breathless – before

diving into another empty
angle and collapsing. Then she sat
up grinning. 'See?' she said.

1. A singer from County Clare

I cast inside my voice,
he said, my land's spirit,
its body, guts, ghost,

its brindling by sun
and cloud on sward, its
tough difficult farms

tucked in sallow nooks
among karst mountains
flecked grey and black,

its goose ponds and mud,
its angles of slopes between
dune-marram and ocean,

flickering waves' duration
and ungraspable curvature
of wicked-angled bays

where gannets dive. These,
he said, wake in my voice
and constitute its timbre.

fulfilling   *will-less will*

2. Way, road, creode

A cultivated field would
yield a surer harvest. One never
before tilled risks wasting time.

Follow a well-worn path and
you might win smoother comfort –
and favour, fame, recognition.

But the way you've chosen
hasn't yet been trodden. There
are no grooves or furrows.

See, unpocked by ruts or
runnels, treads of pioneers,
it isn't even yet a path. But

if it does turn into a high-
way, it will take its directions
from those made by you

who trod and marked it first
in slow, quiet, patient solitude,
working your way, trusting.

---

not investing in sureties   *trusting the way of heaven*

3. A twist

My friend has had
an accident. His bicycle
crashed. He wore

no helmet. His clear
handsome face is now
scarred for good. He

writes: 'It gives a new
philosophical twist to my
outlook on life. During

the operation and in
hospital I was forced
to open one eye and

close the other.' Now
healing, again he opens
both eyes and sees

outward and inward.
A twist. A turn. A turning.
A returning.

4. Tracks to stars and back

Complex thoughts,
many-dimensioned, fling
tracks to stars and back.

'I' dissolves. 'I' keeps
on dissolving. That's hard at
first. But better that way.

When all's said and done,
'I' matters little to anyone.
Least of all you. Winds

go on blowing through
cracks in windows and
walls. Map-based

logistics haunt views
with thunderings not to
be fulfilled. Speckled

words contemplated
in quietness soon return
thoughts to nothing.

5. Alexander calling

2½ year-old Alexander
tells me on the phone he
loves Grandad and he's

drinking from a blue mug
and he seed a butterfly and
there was a slimy slug

in the house and Daddy
did chuck it in the bushes
and in the garden he did

see a blue bottle fly and
a big bumble bee and Zigzag
(tabby cat) did

chase a frog and
the frog was green and
no he not coming to

Grandad's house today
coz he did come yesterday
and goodbye Grandad.

6. The clown

At half past nothing
the things in the mind begin
to change shape or dissolve.

'You need to make a razor-
sharp break with the future
to open up anything in the

now of dancing,' intones
the Dramaturg. The clown
curtsies profusely, licks

his orange and lemon
flavoured lollipop and
sticks it upside-down

in the Dramaturg's breast-
pocket. 'Monsieur,' he whispers
in the latter's ear, 'my work,

my art, the nothing of nothing,
is to follow – wherever this scuds
or sails – into nothing at all.'

Big Blessing, Possessing

---

mountain   *astride heaven*

Cox's Pippin

I bring you the very
sweetest apple in the whole
world from an orchard

in England. Its pips
rattling in their pods recall
spring rain scattering

on greeny rivers. Red,
umber and gold clouds
on its shiny skin bring

back misted dawns
and bronzed sunsets of
English summers.

The bitter-sweet taste
of its pale flesh crunched
against teeth and tongue

comes back to you
from the far paradisal
side of childhood.

1. Thesaurus

The pleasures of secondhand shops
on Mill Rd have been mine for 35 years:
Cambridge Resale, where for £29.99, I

bought my sleek fine-tuned ghetto-
blaster, on which I still play obsolete
audio-cassettes; the *Salvation Army*,

where in 1987 I found a serviceable
suit for ten pounds, wearing which I
later met ambassadors, a president

and a duke; *Cornwall's*, from whom
I built a collection of patterned plates
from post-mortem house-clearouts;

And the *RSPCA bookshop*, where
for peanuts I unearthed half a dozen
dictionaries, by now dog-eared and

finger-marked. These pleasures I
praise and sing. May those who provide
them live in health and joy for ever.

---

put aside your spiritual tortoise   *and stop drooling*

2. Still and on

May this work
move on, and on
its winding way

and these words
hold well together
and, in their time

wherever they
carry, together
hold constant

at all points
on this narrow strip
between blindness

and sight, pain
and joys, water
and water, stardust

and earthdust
void and air
fire and fire.

---

a wagon-axle bracket   *comes off, mend it*

3. A maze book

A maze book, camouflaged
for the undazed, unbenighted,
in corners of any voice,

caped, capped, canopied,
odyssified and penelopied
by its own solutions –

a knit-stitched-sewn book
morninged and eveninged,
still and always *kinging* –

an everywhere-and-
nowhere book, legibly
copied in mirrors

whose dawns jingle and
dangle, here, in this corner-
terraced house at

three roads' intersection –
Argyle Street, Charles Street,
Stockwell Street.

4. Behind the bean stalks

When George glimpsed
the small dragon skulking
semi-coiled behind

the bean stalks at the
far end of the garden, he
wondered whose human

expression he'd caught
and half-recognised passing
across its monster face.

Was it his mother's or
his uncle's or his father's
or his own? When he

glanced back he saw no
resemblances. The creature
lay sprawled full

length among cabbages,
beet and leeks, mouth wide
in a grin, snoring.

a young bull   *horns buffered*

5. Jade cup

'A concentrated, laconic,
lapidary quality, making
an impression of austere

elegance, pith and virility,
unequalled in any other
invented instrument of

human communication.'
So Joseph Needham *aka*
Li Yuese sums up the

Chinese language near
the start of his 24-volume
masterpiece, *Science and*

Civilisation in China.
Could this approximating
clay English, despite

flaws, gaps and holes,
ever aspire to such jade-
engraved perfection?

6. Ground, grounds, store

Human speech   surfaces
from oceanic language first
through dreaming.

Phonemes   root and
grow on binary distinctions
built in the mouth's cave.

Speaking   the quick
exterior human dialogue
opens now in now.

Writing   miming speech
through time throughout it
makes it monumental.

Lettered   word and
ideogram spatialising history
treat and draw time as field.

Poetry   inner speech
pouring from such stores
roams earth and vast skies.

(27)

Nourishing

---

thunder   *under mountain*

Summer, svemir

On our big round table
a vase of campanula. On
our small table a potted

flowering hibiscus. On
windowsills, four orchids –
two speckled, one white,

one pink. Outside,
two doves sit side-by-side
in our rowan-tree.

Our bowl has been
replenished, our cup
overflows with juices

and still this singular
flood pours in and
through us. Today

our lives are
a garden. Nothing
doesn't cohere.

1. Harriet, queue-jumping

Impatient to get home
and cook the scrumptiously
large lobster currently

garlanded in parsley,
stranded among ice blocks
and displayed on

its sloping slab of
marble, above haddock
kippers prawns mullet

cod plaice scab crayfish
mussels cockles whelks oysters
sea-bass salmon trout herring

and mackerel, Harriet
managed to jump the queue of
hatted women that sloped

all the way up the hill
from the fishmonger
to the post office.

mouth-watering   *drooling*

2. Walking companion

Turning the corner of
Stockwell St into Mill Rd
I met a skeleton and

we walked west
towards Parker's Piece
together, chatting

affably. He was on
his way to a meeting in
the Town Hall and I

to buy apples, pears,
beetroot and artichokes
in the market. He

didn't speak but
his few words formed
clear in my head as

we walked. Later,
back home, he nodded and
grinned in my mirror.

3. Oh my (our) country

Oh my (our) country, replete
with privileges and snobberies
accumulated over centuries,

laid out in every enclosed
and cultivated land-parcelling,
built into wall and roof,

plotted, mapped, chartered
into every street, and separated,
clustered, reamed, piled in

by and through minds of every
mature well-trained disciplined
inhabitant, what scope do you

offer of fair chance? Since your
walls, fences, hedges, ditches block
him, her, us, each other in/out,

your mad sales and purchasings
on beauty behind bodymind barriers
demoralise age, destroy youth.

stay put   *not yet time to cross the great water*

4. On feeding

Who is to feed whom
when? That the living
feed the living

is the law of modest
mothers, that the living
feed the dying

the law of mercy's
ministrants, that the dead
feed the living, law of

meat and matter, that
the living feed the dead,
law of remembrance

and mourning, the dying
feed the living, law of
mist and memory

and the dead feed
the dead, of mortality
and immortality.

nourished from below   *in-formed from above*

5. Wild strawberry

Cling to the rock
as if you were the root
of a wild strawberry

clasping tendrils
among crannies in
the cliff-face

over lake-waters,
and hang your leaves
direct from heaven

in a nook where
daylight and darkness
both nourish you

and no huge winds
reach, where you've all
time and space

to grow and lead
your own sweet red
wild strawberry life.

nourished from above   *growing deeper down*

6. Apple

The last thing he dreamed of
was digging a small hole, half a
metre across, one metre deep,

and layering it with loam
in the quiet walled courtyard
seven paces from the door

behind his own familiar house,
which, outside the dream, he knew
wasn't his at all, at the edge

of the village in Serbia, which
in the dream was his home, though
outside sleep and death, he had

never lived there, never would –
and on the layer of loam, placing
a healthy, rounded, pink apple,

covering soil over it, packing it
lightly down, and carefully prodding
a stake in, to mark its position.

(28)

Overbrimming

---

water   *over wood*

The lake rises above the trees

Rain on rain, storm
on storm, flood on
flood. Won't it ever

stop? The only way
forward is this clumsy
paddling, this careful

wading, weighed down
by too much baggage,
and then this slow

laborious scrabbling
from one secured mark
to the next. No time

to contemplate gifts or
horizons, let alone dream
or think. Every muscle,

bone, corpuscle, must
be put to work, getting
past and through.

flooded over   *withdraw, move on*

1. Building a tabernacle

Build it in remembrance and
celebration as a shack or booth
beside your house. Construct

its roof as a trellis open to sky
twined with branches of myrtle,
brookside willow, vine, and

leaves of palm, orange and lemon.
Inside the thatch, from walls, rafters
and doorposts, hang plums, dates,

pomegranates, apples. Strew
its floor with mats of rushes and
wild grasses. From fine-ground

flour, bake a dozen cakes. Light
lamps with wicks dipped in olive oil
and at evening serve your children

pastries and fruit. Then let them
sleep in the tabernacle. Above, may
they glimpse patched starlight.

weave mats   *for the floor*

2. Old willow

By the stream an old
willow is sprouting we
thought had dried up.

The widower who lived
on the hill at the far end
of the track leading

up to the high plains
has come down to our
village and taken a

neighbour's eldest
brightest daughter
as wife. Both now

wear fat smiles.
Her belly is already
rounding nicely.

She is tall, strong,
and firm-breasted. She
will inherit his land.

---

a withered tree   *grows new shoots*

3. The minister has been tainted

The minister has been
tainted. When his wife
was told, she fainted.

Yes I do suppose
it's possible he's not the
monster he's painted.

Our consciences
are a riddle. Look, who
isn't on the fiddle?

The pole across the
abyss sags to breaking
point in the middle.

The emperor has lost
control. This country leaks
like a cracked bowl.

So get thee into
exile, mate. And try
to save your soul.

the girder holding the roof up   *sags*

4. Quake

Our roof may fall in. Panic
multiplies – too fast for response,
too sudden for remedy.

Growls, roars, tremors
between tectonic plates. Cracks
in earth's mantle.

How shall we avoid yet
another calamity? Foundations
need scaffolding,

deepening, shoring, and
roots of pillars, drilling like
teeth. Diagonal trusses

and cross braces will
buttress frame and shell.
Nor shall we rely

on others to get
these tasks done. We'll see
to them ourselves. Now.

---

beams creak, girders sag   *cracks appear in walls*

5. Letter from Court

Our Empress has taken an even
younger lover. She found her last
locked in a lady-in-waiting's arms.

Graciously she dismissed both from
court, with settlements typical of her
generosity. Her new beau, a Hussar,

is possessed of excellent saddle-
skills and evidently endowed with
promise. Vetted by her Majesty's

most seasoned aide (Mistress-of-
the-Chamber), he is said to be not
wanting in enthusiasm or talent.

So, Emilia, dearest cousin, although
past childbearing, our Empress truly
blossoms. Shuvalov says this year's

harvest will yield a bumper crop.
I trust you are practising your divine
spinet. My greetings to your Father.

a withered willow   *puts out yellow blossoms*

6. Floods

Roads at hills' feet swirl
and in valleys' lowest dips
cross-currents carve

runnels down
to our river, swollen five
times normal width.

Thick sludge swirls,
fast moving, covering
tree trunks, whose

greeneries swish away.
We've stabled our horses
on higher land, but

our cows, marooned
in corners of sodden fields,
cluster wherever small

pockets of green have
not yet gone under. We
can't cross the river.

water overhead　　　　　　　　　　　　　　*river overbrimming*

(29)

Falling
(in a Pit)

---

water   *water*

Way down

If all ways are
gifts, named or unnamed,
downwards may yield

dark treasure,
though it is called
unnameable, being

so swift sweep-
ing in arrival, no
recognizance can

prepare the heart
for batterings there
to be endured.

From retrospects
you'll know later
were no accidents,

courage. What is
yet indecipherable, you
will mark and name.

---

jeopardy   *in double danger*

1. Tazmamart

8 July 1973, Rabat,
Morocco: Ali Bourequat and
two of his five brothers

Bayazid and Midhat, are
arrested and interrogated
blindfold in presence

of Hassid, King of
Morocco, who wants them
out of his damn way.

They get incarcerated
for eighteen years, the last
eleven in Tazmamart,

a disused tank barracks
beneath Atlas Mountains.
They get holed up in

adjacent underground
cells, three meters by two
pitch dark.

already in the abyss   *and falling into a pit*

2. Where four winds meet

Never allowed out,
not seeing daylight for
eighteen years, each

has a concrete slab
for bed, eighty centimetres
long, two or three

blankets regardless
of heat or cold and one
change of shirt and

trousers per year. With
scorpions, cockroaches
and two visiting snakes

as cellmates, they
learn to sleep sitting.
If they lie down,

they'll never get up
or out of this desert hole
where four winds meet.

---

3. With their whole hearts

Through ventilation-holes
they call each other, chant
Koranic verses, share

memories of paradisal
Paris streets, bars and cafés
where they'd met to drink

and restaurants where they'd
dined. They convert chick-pea
gruel to princely feasts

and, together, map contours
of countless remembered and
imagined places, name them

and take walks there, inhabiting
and repossessing them with their
whole hearts. 'So long as we

had nothing at all,' says Ali,
'our memories clothed us, who
were spiritually naked.'

4. Torturers

They supported one another.
Not knowing if they'd ever get
out, they did not give up.

When unseen companions
in neighbouring cells died, they
mourned them with prayers.

Deaths of others, together
with overhanging presences of
their own, redoubled their

strengths, for these were
inverse to those of emperors
and kings: the powers

of being powerless being
doubly more durable. Later
Ali says, 'Human beings

possess resources they don't
know about. Torturers can't
destroy a person's dignity.'

---

handed through the vent   *a bowl of rice*

5. An owl

Then an owl comes, bird
of ill-omen for Moslems. Each
nightfall seven times the

creature of night cries its
other cry, not the death cry.
5 September 1991: release,

no less mysterious and
incomprehensible than first
arrest and imprisonment.

Each weighs half his
previous body weight and
has to relearn to walk

and see. In this new light,
things keep flickering and
blurring then going out

of focus and dazzling
unbearably. Vision takes
three months to stabilise.

pit full   *but an outside does exist*

6. By a Scandinavian sea

Ali walks on the beach
by a Scandinavian sea
and picks up pebbles.

'I no longer know what
fear is,' he says. 'And death
doesn't frighten me. Or

violence. Or threats. I've
been plated in an armour
that isn't known to exist

and can't be taken off.
I'm sharper in awareness
of injustice from knowing

unbounded strength far
beyond hate. We were dead
and we came back. Now

delivered, I savour
unique moment's breath
night and morning.'

(30)

Clinging

Over whole skies

No fire flames once.
That which is bright
happens twice. Sunset

and dawn repeat their
blaze over entire skies
in glory. When flame

clings to the palpable
it connects the world
with invisible power

shattering mountains
to memory, graveyards
into present gardens

and flaring where
boundaries of May trees
bloom white snows.

When brightness clings
to brightness, nothing
happens alone.

fire   brightness doubled

1. Dust speck

Big fat dust speck sits on a blue
felt carpeting square, three feet be-
fore my lowered eyes. We hold

a long duologue, dust speck and
I. Good morning. I focus on you,
dust speck, and you blur in and

out of my head. You expand into
a face and laugh at me. Well, why not.
You shrink, shimmer, turn into a

human eye, fern-frond, poisonous
mushroom, snow-capped mountain I'm
compelled to climb endlessly. You

chase me and whoever-I-is escapes.
You call me back. Dust speck, thank you.
You're mine, I'm yours, you're me,

I'm you. My own anybody's dust
speck, you're filled with scintillating
light. I simply adore you.

2. In the desert (3)

In the desert, belts
of yellow dust encircle
her waist. Dunes

twine her whirled
coiled hair. Termites
scurry across floors

she lies on, waiting
for her to rise, if ever
she will deign so

and the white light
and the black light
beat down, locked

in each other's arms
hardening and softening
into each other. You

are mine, she moans
in whirling wind, although
her speech is wordless.

yellow light   *yellow garment*

3. Indelible shadows tattooed

As sun goes down
mountain's ankles angle
and crush valley treetops.

But at day-end also lurk
shades that won't fade so fast.
Feet of monstrous empires

that marched and galloped
iron-shod across continents
have hammered shadows

through history no wash
or polish can clean or paint
stain or conceal. Visit any

child's nightmares, if you
can ever enter, for a swift
vivid tour. Though not

yet drowned in dark, we
are among those who wear
indelible shadows tattooed.

Sonnenuntergangstraurigkeit   *sighing in sorrow for old age*

4. Towards my window

It's light that
most demands to be
affirmed against

death, and every
body (thing, being) it lands
and sits on and sets

quivering, shimmering –
like these two girls walking
this crunchy-gravelled

path towards my
window, who now sheer
away, left, and are gone –

and these rhododendron
buds clustering against glass,
and these folds in silver-

grey curtains, and these
dried rain specks collecting
dust against panes.

---

it flares suddenly   *then dies down*

5. Untouchable light, miraculous air

Air keeps spilling
out of this world
onto death, almost

as if it were water
from a leaking tap and
time were the wooden

floor it dripped and spilled
onto and soaked through
and trickled between planks

to puddle and pool down
in cellars and stream through
soil onto impermeable

rock. Since this un-
touchable miraculous
air that slips through my

lungs will suddenly be
taken from me, I drink it
all the more joyfully.

---

light pouring   *no tearfloods nor sigh-tempests*

6. No horizon at Trabzen

Light breaks immaculate
day each day. Dawn's brazen
virginity, repeatedly un-

repeatable, lifts even a
battered and recalcitrant heart,
astonishes intellect, impels

wonder along bloodstream,
pours depth and longing into and
through breath, re-establishes

hope in bones' deepest portals.
Light, most loved, untouchable,
shared secret that all

most cherish and adore –
here at Trabzen, over hills
and minarets, you rise as

everywhere majestic and
decisive above dispersing
mist-veils, mist-curtains.

---

light   *majestic, decisive*

(31)

Reciprocating

---

a lake   *on a mountain*

A lake on a mountain

Massing water
presses down, finding
lowest outlet. A lake

collects, builds
in deepest possible
places, soaks

into permeable
ground to pool on
impassable rock.

A mountain presses
up, pushes its presence
to rear, bucking

against gravity. So
when a lake forms on
a mountain, opposed

forces meet and
merge in fine self-
checking balance.

gentle above   *firm below*

1. Gates inside gates

Last year, mere children –
these nights they will not
want sleep. Need is now

to explore, to be explored,
each an ocean, a continent
to the other. They cling

mouths, stroke flesh, dig,
dip, drive into each other,
and that's all that matters.

No wonder they have
forgotten friends, parents,
teachers. What happens

now is finer far than
anything, and however long
now may last, irrelevant.

Now gates inside gates
open, close, close, open,
re-open, open, open.

2. Plan A

He dreamed a plan.
His plan dreamed him.
His dream told him

all, of itself, in detail.
He woke, remembering it,
He wrote it all down.

His plan was perfect.
He rushed out, enthusing.
He spoke to the wind

then rushed back in.
Wind bubbled through him.
He told everyone about it.

He took it for granted
all would listen. And love it.
And love *him*. And follow.

But everyone looked
the other way. He was ready.
Nobody else was.

---

need   *knock-kneed*

2. Plan B

He dreamed a plan.
His plan dreamed him. He
woke and remembered it.

He wrote it all down
then hesitated. He drew
the wind towards him

which was not impressed
and blew more chaotically
in a hundred directions.

He saw his dream fallible
and his perfect plan after
all not so perfect. So

he slept on his dream,
refined it. And waited.
Others came, bearing

the same dream-plan as
his. Everyone agreed. His
dream, his way, was ours.

---

non-action   *still and active*

4. Unpredictable heart

He paces up and
down. Uncertain. Out
of harmony. His

mind, his hesitator, sets
him thinking. Too much.
To be without thought

might notch a finer key.
Everybody watches him
but nobody will follow

until he follows his own
quick heart and feeds his
being with constancy.

When two crystal
glasses chime, they keep
constant note and tone.

Accord grows
on their tuning
wave on wave.

---

5. Words for a *hamsah*

Whoever would beset
with falsities or falsenesss
the bearer of this hand

keeper of this heart
guardian of these eyes
opener of these lips

tuner of these ears
sensor of these nostrils
teller of this tongue

cleaver of these teeth
bearer of these shoulders
conductor of this mind

tiller of this belly
master of these legs
leader of these feet

angel of this groin –
if there be such a one
let him or her beware.

6. Mutual respect

Both leaders promised co-
operation and unity in a coalition
based not on strict agendas or

self-interest but a true meeting
of minds of two men of integrity
committed to an accord

weightier than compromise –
which would blend differing though
compatible views in mutual

respect, both parties being
bent on (devoted to) the (whole)
country's good. So they ironed

out differences, delivered
fine-tuned speeches, and shaped
and shared power. Till it irked.

Apparently tricking themselves to
believe in their own false sincerities,
they failed to fool their followers.

reciprocating   *on jaws, cheeks, tongues*

(32)

Enduring

Between is and not

That which is
nameless and formless
is, by definition, not.

Its condition being
not-being, what-it-is
is *what-is-not*.

It can't be approached
or encompassed, because
what-it-is is not.

Nor can its notness
be present, because it
contradicts isness.

Yet though absent, by
mere dint of being called,
notness is *ever-present*.

In continuous interplay
between isness and notness
arises this. Enduring.

ever-changing　　　　　　道　　　　　　*always enduring*

256

1. Working at it

The start is hardest.
To get it to work well
not only volitions

but also a slow quiet
patience and maintained
attentiveness are

crucial parts of its
making. This is what
the book says of

and about itself. Slender
your chances for growing
upwards and outwards

unless you happen on
the crack among cloud
that will allow

intention to pierce
through. Work not only
at it but *with* it, *for* it.

2. The way you chose

The way you chose
chose you. You and it
are one in both

will and volition,
response and reply,
quest and question.

The way moves
you, moves through you
ever-changing, always

one. It gathers you,
gathers in you. It *is* you
in doing and being.

It could have been no
other way, past regret,
now a mist dissolved.

Between *not* and *is*
you steer, keeping to
the central way.

---

between not and is   中道   *regret vanishes*

3. Your name

Your name was a door
I walked through. Now
it's a wall my fingers

scrape until they're
bloodied. And now it's
a room with no lights

and no windows
hermetically sealed. And
now, it's a hole opening

in the cell floor I fall
and fall through to the
other side – of what?

See how slow and
sure I glide. See my organs
wings. And you, little

fish I once plunged for –
nameless invisible fish in
deepest darkest ocean.

4. Who list to hunt

No crows and no scare-
crows on these fields. No grain.
Hardly a husk left over.

Gleaning with harvesters
and guns, landlords have cleaned
out more or less everything.

Try knolls at fields' edges.
No hint of burrow or warren,
no loose soil but anthills.

Try woods. No boar or
deer linger, even though
you hide and wait ages.

No grouse on moor or
by forest edge. No pheasants
in marsh or spinney.

No place to find or
feed anybody. Time to
get out, move on.

fainting I follow   *I leave off therefore*

5. Field work

He works, walks, wakes
in interconnecting fields. Through
them he thinks, speaks, dreams.

To him, all fields form one
multidimensional field, infinite
in scope and variety. And all

he is and perceives, through
all seven senses, merges, fits,
blends in, with, all else. So

his doing is extension and part
of this all-embracing coherence.
Borders and barriers blur, all

edges are doors, all frontiers
are to be crossed, and all vistas
provisional and temporary.

Ideas are light-filled as flowers,
flowers deep as ideas, and both
breathe wonder and miracle.

vision gentle   *perspectives clear, well-founded*

6. Morrow

Where I'll be going,
she said, is uncertain
with or without you.

Several of the puppets
you dangled looked
almost human.

Their eyelids fluttered
and their hands flexed,
unflexed and flexed

pretty much like mine.
Eyes creasing, she smiled
into French: *Le futur*

tu sais, n'est pas l'avenir.
I wonder who will be
accompanying whom

on the long journey
called *morrow*, unstoppable,
unreachable.

agitated   *time to move on*

(33)

Retreating

Moses

Old man, longbeard, sits
on boulder gazing up at Sinai
shrouded under cloud.

How did he climb that
crag? Fly? Or ferried on
a desert eagle's back?

Forty days, forty nights
on the mountain, alone in
the Presence. He carried

down two stone tablets
one under each arm, chiselled
before his eyes, it's said

by the Lord's right hand
directing his. What I shan't
forget is wells of black light

in fathomless eyes, face
shining, skin a young man's
swathed in blue haze.

1. Tail-end stragglers

Our forerunners got through
or perished. We stragglers were
trapped on three sides by

chasers, and on our fourth
by mountains. Evening fell.
We rested. Several wormed

away on bellies down
to find a river. We few left
among shadows kept

very quiet. Night thickened.
We merged into it, identifying
with blackness, snatching

what scant sleep we could.
By mid-morning our pursuers
had evaporated into valleys.

Time now to retreat even
further, to find space higher
on one of those mountains.

retreating at the tail-end   *somewhere to go*

2. Holding fast

Who would have believed
this wiry, darting-eyed man
strong and supple enough

to throw ten opponents
twice his size and not blink
eye or strain muscle?

He honed his masteries
meditating months as a hermit
in a high mountain cave.

His old skin has browned,
yellowed, grown pliant again
like earth under rain,

as if protected by an
invisible cloak, an extra skin
in which his self, its sole

occupant, mindfully,
fills every fibre and pore
and, mindlessly, empties.

---

wearing a yellow ox-hide   *no-one is able to loosen*

3. Must, ought

Eyes down-inclining,
I entered in here-now,
in their intertwining.

What might interfere
or come undermining
but a host of sincere

wanderings of thought
commenting and resisting
on this *must*, that *ought*,

clamouring, insisting,
till skin and muscles fought
and clarities kept misting?

How I despised
myself and all I am –
all I had prized

ham scam sham.
Squatting, self-paralysed.
should I give a damn?

retreating from dark   *carrying dark inside*

4. Split off

Then some bits of us
got split off and went on
living outside and

without us. Where they
evolved. Took on shapes
we wouldn't recognise

as living. But shared
so much of our DNA they
could have actually

been us. Wizened multi-
legged squelchy creatures,
each smaller than a

five-year-old child's foot,
thousands of them careering
downhill, above our house,

relentlessly focused on
us, galloping, tumbling one
over another, towards us.

retreating unready   *bits of dark split off*

5. Retreating

During the Cultural Revolution
Buddhist monasteries were the least
safe places of all. Xiao Yao, aged

nearly 80, master of martial arts,
healing, meditation, left Jiuyi temple
perched on its white-clouded

peak, to live as a hermit, then
wandered along Xiang River, until
he reached Xiangtan. At a resort

for party officials, he got a job
as boiler attendant, always on call,
managing and stoking furnaces.

Calling himself Mr. Tan, he slept
on a mattress in the boiler room. So,
incognito, Xiao Yao retreated

from his mountain retreat to find
safer retreat in the city, by the river,
servant to the blazing heart of fire.

6. In Epping Forest

Jing walks his border collie
in Epping Forest, throwing
sticks for his dog to catch.

Under an oak he sits
to meditate. Collie rests on
forepaws and haunches.

Lone walkers, children,
couples pass. A boy calls,
'Oy, aintcha cold, mister?'

Smiles open and spread
through him, then join up
a single smile.

Stepping on his right
shoulder, a squirrel leaps
from ground to tree.

A heron swoops
to her fish pool, breaking
her own reflection.

---

cool, still   *bonded but unbounded*

Powering

---

thunder   *over heaven*

Tree

Huge, beautiful, noble tree,
vertical broad-diametered trunk
earth-keeled, sky-bound,

with many-handed woody
knuckles, root-fingers, rock-
grasping, mineral-tapping,

drawing subterranean streams,
intertwined, tangling unseen seams,
rain-soaked, storm-braving tree,

gravity-centre solid and low,
sturdy-standing, balanced, poised,
mast swaying under thunder,

your finest and most intricate
leaf-and-blossom-bearing fronds
stretch to touch high heaven

while your whole body dances,
billowing, bending, swaying, green
hair, gold aura, streaming wind.

firm in movement   *moving in stillness*

1. A good general

A strong swimmer in
swirling currents, he saved
eight others from

drowning as they crossed
two rivers, fleeing their bombed
village. Three more

perished, shot, crossing
scrubland, including his
younger brother. The

six who came through lay
and wept beneath bushes and
in crevasses. That night

he sat apart, back against
a cliff-face, saying nothing,
watching stars. Once over

the border he drilled and
disciplined his men, taught
them skills of killing.

2. A modest man

No charismatic
demagogue, he made sure
first to look after his

own and hone their
judgements and speeds
in strategy. He

deepened their
trusts and loyalties, not
only to himself but

one another. They repaid
him by following and
honouring him all his

life long. Strangers
said it was they who made
him a good general.

To his end he remained
modest, with a dry
understated humour.

3. A charismatic leader

Is a charismatic leader a
blessing or misfortune for his
people? He saps thought,

their thought. He assumes it
as a mantle. He makes decisions
for them, their decisions. He

takes on their troubles. He
releases them from responsibility
from thinking too much, if at all.

He saves them time, money,
anxiety, even from themselves.
Thanks to their loyalty, faith,

and devotion, he may one
day be declared transcendental,
immortal, a saint, an avatar,

a heavenly god, son of the
living God, etc., even though
like us, he shits and will die.

---

a weakling uses force   *a powerful person doesn't*

4. Levers behind the panel

Hearing an unknown prisoner being
tortured in the cell next to his own, Mikis
Theodorakis tapped on the wall between –

There are two of us. There are three of us.
There are a thousand and thirteen of us. So
the world is regulated and sustained

by huge numbers of people acting
alone or in tiny groups who, with no
particular claim to special merit

or distinction, behave not only with
common decency but heroic courage
and compassion, especially in times

of upheaval. Those who claim control
over events by manipulating power strut
about in alluring limelight, never quite

realising the levers behind the panel
aren't in their grasp at all but in the hands
of quite ordinary people, like us.

---

there's no discouragement   *can make him once relent*

5. Thirty-six just men

Thirty-six just men at any one time
stalk injustice in the world. When one dies
another is born. Nobody knows where.

If you think there's no justice, wait
till you hear of one or, if you're very
lucky, meet one. It 'furthers' to seek

out such a man. Your entire life may
be transformed. To be touched by him,
to look in his eyes as he sees into yours

may mean shadows rolling away
at least for a while. But remember you
may not recognise or notice him. He

walks quietly and on most occasions
doesn't look or act differently from you.
Remember too, whatever he is and has

to give you isn't release from troubles
but your taking on your own life, work
for what you do and claim and are.

---

not strong oneself   *borrowing other's strengths*

6. Past zenith

Once clock hands
flicker past zenith,
strengths wane.

Expansive and
expensive fields of
upkeep shrink.

No time for butting
and shoving. What's
needed next is quiet

doing not getting,
being not begetting,
more allowing,

less loud calling,
calm standing back
and making way

at the finishing
in unfettered joy
undiminishing.

---

after all the iffing and butting   *good fortune*

(35)

Dawning

fire   *over the earth*

At an oblique angle

At an oblique angle
to the eastern side of
tomorrow, and

of expected shadow,
the remit, constant,
remains, extends:

to unhook perfections
from scaffolds they've
been hanged on,

coils they've been
sprung in, wound
and interwound,

join fires tumbling
like waterfalls with
up-flowing streams,

unfold not-yet-seen
pleats interlayering
dark and morning.

the opaque clings   *to the transparent*

1. Dawn

Dawn lay
mother of pearl
below rooftops.

Trees
in purple robes
lined their avenues.

Mists pillowed
the hills like
quiet sheep.

Without lifting
a finger, light
unlocked the gardens.

Window panes
glistened in dew
when day breathed

on them. Glory
hung all over
the air.

calm and unhurried   *in its own time*

2. I part the curtains

I part the curtains
a child again. And even
though long gone over

to the other side, and
you still being *here,* not
there – again I see you

alive and breathing, and
dizzied by your perfume,
smell your kind breath,

scent your hollows. And
again inside you alone naked
breathe and am born

and reborn and Glory
sing to have known you
your body-of-bodies

your breasts your hands
your fine sparkling mind
your wise gentle eyes.

3. Light and things

How light and things
trust each other. Unshakeably.
Light every day loves

things so much it sticks
to, passes through, lingers
over, surrounds

all. Light adheres, inheres
everywhere, there, here, in
here. Bathed, swathed

in light, things become
themselves the more, the most.
You know this always

the way it is, was, ways
they be. Between light and
things, every moving

moment calls out glory un-
repeatable, sheen inseparable
from either or both.

with trust, things   *shine in the now*

4. Morning, open windows

Sunlight is flickering
on the wall facing
the long window

in our sitting room
and the leaves
of houseplants

on the windowsill
scatter their magnified
shadows there

daubing and splashing
the whole wall,
bathing and swathing

the entire interior
in singular
unrepeatable

patterned waves
where nothing can
or will keep still.

---

scurrying like a mouse   *leaping like a squirrel*

5. Dawn will come and have your eyes

Dawn will come
and have your eyes
brown-eyed

woman of marshes
green-eyed
woman of rivers

in pleated robes
yellow-streaked
purple-corded

gold-braided
flame-tautened
terror-tightened

spattered in mud
blood and soils
blue-eyed

woman of skies
hemmed in moons
couched in darkness

her light   *will light up every corner of the land*

6. Winter solstice

Sky a frosted pearly
porcelain blue as I walk
down Mill Road this

morning to post a last
Christmas card. A mass
of people out, traffic

honking, blocked solid.
Yesterday I heard another
friend has died – that's

two gone this week.
Today consciousness, life
itself, seems improbable,

miraculous. Presences
of small glories mean more
than all or any of

heaven's promises.
At home I boil a sky
blue egg for lunch.

at the tipping point   *take charge of one's own domain*

(36)

Darkening

---

fire   *beneath the earth*

Meditation at Majdanek

Here not just bodies were
destroyed. Here even souls
were scattered so deep

into waste-pits they
could never re-emerge. So
very small they had been

shrivelled as to be almost
nothing, then pulped more
and then dispersed.

I could not take a pebble
from this place for it would
weigh so heavy in my

pocket as to burn right in
and through my flesh. This
dust is ash of powdered

souls. Memory, mother
of poems, shrinks away
to scream not mourn.

---

crow caws at dusk   *light sinks under the earth*

1. Time of deliverance

Time of deliverance
is not yet come. Still we
are oppressed by the

hugeness of high
ways stretching out
before our histories

ever began, and
puniness of our paths,
their slight span

across light, by
comparison, and
then yet another

equally unthinkable
vastness coming after
and without us. Our

task is not hopeless
nonetheless. We shall
hide our lights. Wait.

2. Under occupation

To save himself and others, he
veiled his words in cunning and
actions in such simplicity

that all thought him mad.
He treated foes and friends alike.
Took care to show everyone

one regular, bland, inane,
smiling face. Avoided lickspittles.
Trusted nobody, not even

those he loved. Never wrote
anything down. Remembered
everything. Moved light, with

few belongings. Stayed calm,
expressionless, silent whenever
possible. If questioned, he

replied, grinning, in riddles. By
then, thought stupid, he kept his
light burning steady. Inward.

---

under black light   *brilliance concealed*

3. Child survivor's testimony

I'm alive because in
the middle of the shooting
my father said, *Go.*

He let go my hand
and pushed my back
like this and said *Go,*

in an ordinary way
as if he was telling me
what to do, as usual.

Go, he said. It
didn't feel special. He
didn't say *Run* or

Go quick, or *Hurry.*
But he turned his face
away to my mother.

I walked away slowly.
Nobody noticed. That's
why I'm alive.

---

gentle in the face of dark   *strong in the jaws of death*

4. Red Cross Hospital, Belsen, after liberation, 1945

The madness is over
but we're still alive, said
the emaciated jeweller

whose forefathers had
set diamonds for Bohemian
kings and queens. Why,

he said, tell me why
have I been spared? Rain
pelted down days,

muddying everything.
Typhus struck. An Irish
nurse fell in love with

a brave Canadian captain.
An English doctor caught
the typhus and died. The

jeweller got to Toronto.
Married. Had children. Taught
Yiddish. Died 1988.

surviving evil   *some emerged into light*

5. 'To write a poem after Auschwitz is barbaric'

I shall find words, my
own, after, despite *and* because
of this. *And* speak of it.

Your call, in words, to
silence, misconstrues what
poems are, do, are for.

To call out love and justice,
born of the heart's oldest and
simplest imperatives – hope,

compassion, courage, truth,
and defiance of death-makers.
Whatever your intent, your

words invite barbarism
to root in nothing-saying.
Failure is not of or in

language, but small trust
and short vision. Our task lives
in words. Not outwith them.

from depths of dark   *to confront and conquer evil*

6. *Tikkun*, Majdanek

Our task, to restore
the fallen. Nothing else or
less. How many shrivel

and perish each time
creatures are slaughtered,
when not mere bodies

are reduced to ash
but spirits pulverised for
ever. A spirit destroyed

does not come back.
Dark powers of such death-
holes spread, infect

breath. Our job, to clean
air, protect unkempt wild
hidden spaces twined

in forest light, where
nest singing birds that
chorus like angels.

Dwelling, Householding

---

wind   *fanning fire*

Home

To inhabit one's own
space at last, to obtain
complete access with

key, by one's very
own work, to cross
debt's threshold,

owing tribute no longer
in rent, tax, insurance
except to the dead

and the unborn, to have
paid off their mortgage
and to stand secure in

one's own experience,
to nourish loved ones
and raise a family

of human voices
across the years —isn't
this worth the doing?

1. Lara's garden in August

Drove Arijana through Friday
rush-hour to stay the weekend
with Lara in her new house

in St. Albans. Jelena arrived
from work and we sat and drank
elderflower cordial and

chilled white wine in the long
garden and looked at old photos
and chattered about

family things, nothing in
particular. Arijana hosed flower
beds, lawn, potted plants,

then I left and drove
back home. Pleasures so
simple they're almost

incommunicable,
fabric of most
people's everything.

2. Ownership

The house you rent
or own owns you.
You are guest

of its walled interior
that welcomed you when
you were a stranger.

The conifer's hundreds
of thousands of days
and the millions

of nights slept by stone
that were poured
into the hard

building of wall,
pillar, lintel, roof
antedate and anticipate

you, present
occupier, sitting
here at your ease.

3. Hospitality

Open now doors
of your memory to
guests uninvited

and unexpected,
living, dead and un-
born – for what

use is a voice,
of being human,
to restrain gifts

on a tight leash,
and to parcel out
gobbets of joy

with this or that
end in mind. You
who were born

for singing and
dancing, yield your
life all you own.

4. Poverty

Wino wreathed
asleep in papers over
subway's grilles

gypsy child
up to shoulders
in waste pit

old man trundling
cardboard boxes on
hand-pulled cart

bag woman
young and wizened
squatting a moment

on flight of steps
in front of Municipal
Palace of Justice

are human as you
and belong by right
with you here

5. Necessity

Crude Necessity
demands this.
It is time to give

and to ask help.
Now is time to
knit and weave

all you know
back in the single
seamless fabric,

forgetting nothing,
ignoring no-one, not
even the poorest.

It is time to act
now. Now is always
time to act. All

beggars are holy
and any time you
too may be one.

6. Small poem for Gully

Your path, you choose,
that chooses you, is good,
honourable and true

for yourself you test
and probe at every step.
Commending that,

what least I ask my-
self is mediation of
perfectionist desire,

attentive to undercurrents
and shadows. In their well-
ings, among interstices, so

long as we keep questioning
each other and ourselves, we
might get through and under

clichés that call, waylay
and even blind us among
blander, lightfilled spaces.

---

sincere and true   *to oneself, with dignity*

(38)

Separating

Sieve

It sifts, sorts
small from large, fine
from small, small

from minuscule. De-
pending on gradations,
its mesh distinguishes

dusts by degrees,
gritty, coarse, grainy,
fine, powdered, etc.

It can prepare
liquid so pure, all but
saturated particles

remove entirely. In
doing its job faithfully,
it operates in

one of two ways:
retains what you value
or allows it through.

1. Chameleon

Regard chameleon – if
you can find him. He was
on branch behind rock

before light below sur-
face inside rain between
morning and evening

(through glistening and
glistening) on star-dot and
through and in blinding

blaze of sun. Catch his
position and you will not
track his movement and

vice-versa. How beauti-
ful chameleon ungraspable
as moment leaping and

in less than whisper less
than breath – gone. And
you? Who might you be?

creature that appears, disappears   *and comes back*

2. To open doors

Is name mere *shadow*? Reality
is not its name, nor are words
names, or shadows, or masks

but doors. Isn't it time to trust
them opened again? And again,
and then again? said my

guide, and smiled. She
looked out through her window.
A blackbird was singing

in a rowan tree. A boy
on a bike, with yellow helmet,
rode by, followed by his dad

in a red helmet. A young
man wearing a green anorak
paused then walked on.

She turned again to me.
Isn't it always time to open doors
of (to) things through words?

---

meeting again   *in a narrow lane*

3. I can't say *you* any more

Our friendship's gone
for good. I can't say *you*
any more. Whatever

person *you* referred to
refuses contact or reference.
When our break came

in shock I refused to
believe it, tried to call
you back, composed

speeches and letters
to an image, memory,
absence, mirage – in

hopeless hope, in empty
longing. Now it's as if we
were dead to each other.

But when I dream of
you (often), you're your very
old self. And 100% alive.

4. Thank you ghost

Thank you ghost
who will be born
then for catching

these in time.
Thank you, you as
yet breathless

for being a
whole moment's
friend. Without

you no poem
and indeed no
word. Solitary

again and again
this stuns itself
against silence

until you
saunter insouciant
into its field.

isolated, meet an initiator   *truth and sincerity fuse*

5. The stone carver

She carves stone as
a knife bites through a
loaf. As if the rough

unhewn block gave
scant resistance to her
chisel's bite. And hard-

edged borders between
stone and air were easy
tracks for her hands

to cross. And her swift
spirit through hands to
probe, to sift, to clear,

and, caring, patient,
to rediscover. As if such
acts of clean separation

rejoined, remoulded
and unfolded original
and originary ways.

---

as if biting tender meat   *ease, speed, resonance*

6. Dusts

She's cleaned her house
and cleaned it again. Dust
blows back in, a swarm

of invisible, magical
creatures, almost angelic,
smothering everything

yet again. Dust in cities
settles on the brain. Dust in
libraries flickers on light.

Sometimes you catch a
(the) moment, you really do,
don't you? But then, what

was it – dust, a nothing,
or figment of a nothing?
It's dust particles model

and mould rooms and
dooms. They plaster and
flake walls of our time.

---

covered in dirt, was that   *an intruder or guest*

(39)

Struggling, Stumbling

---

water   *on the mountain*

Ledge

This is no place to rest one
moment longer than you can
help it. No way forward

or upward. No space for
standing, let alone tent or
fire, to protect you from

all-penetrating shadow
of rock-face, higher than
you've ever clambered,

ragged lash and howl of
curling wind and non-stop
drip-drip of water. Hard

enough struggling up to
this slippery ice-ravaged
cascade-battered ledge.

Harder still to climb back.
Will you keep scrabbling up?
Keep still? Or come down?

1. Danger

Snow lies thick
on the passes. In
a fine grip, ice

binds local roads.
A sadist lover, wind
lashes bare trees.

All wires are down,
broken. Neighbours
intent on their own

survival, heads bent
against this blizzard,
can't be relied on.

Nothing will work but
patience. Don't travel
anywhere, far or near.

Shutter windows.
Keep draughts out. Stay
home. Stoke your fire.

no way forward yet   *better wait, keep still*

2. Minister

When goings got tough, it
would have been easier, safer,
and his family would have

preferred it, had he made
overtures to the others, gone
over to them, embraced

their cause, or at least
allowed them to claim his
approval, even just use

his name. He refused any
such way out through parley.
Instead, quiet-voiced, he

stated his reasons for
not supporting them, re-
pivoted public opinion,

and ensured their plausible
claims and attempted coup
got firmly, finally quashed.

loyal minister   *in tough spot*

3. Toothache

At work as usual in World Trade
Center's South Tower, Sept 10, Jodi
had a mild but gnawing toothache,

so called her dentist and, early
next morning, had a filling done in
a left lower molar. After treatment,

feeling weak, she took a cab home
to rest instead of going to work. And
so escaped death that day. Curious

how apparently unexceptional people
unwittingly find themselves caught up –
or not caught up – in world-shaking

dramas, turning points in history, by
one small twist out of normal routine.
Hard, too, to put aside imponderable

questions of identity and destiny,
how they interact, when it comes to an
apparent coincidence saving a life.

forward, danger   *back, safety*

4. Becket

He knew both options in advance.
To have ridden to court and made up
with the King, on the King's terms,

might have meant a way out, of
a kind, but not even physical safety
could be guaranteed now. And

besides, that way taken would
have meant ethical collapse, be-
trayal, not of friendship but of

deeper, higher codes – which
he couldn't have lived with. Too late
anyway, for such compromises.

Even so, to stay in Canterbury in-
evitably meant a long slow wait for
Death's ministers to discharge

their final sword-stabs and dagger-
cuts through his brave weary heart.
He had no choice but stay.

---

his basic nature   *tells him, this way*

5. Warsaw Ghetto, April-May 1943

Some fought back. Most were
destroyed. Few survived. Remember
and honour them

all who perished. There was
nowhere to go. Young, brave, they
networked tunnels and dugouts

across the Ghetto. On Passover-
Eve, April 19, Muranowski Square,
they ambushed an SS troop and

captured guns. Flew two flags –
Polish and Star of David – to fly side
by side from rooftops four days.

Nazis set the whole Ghetto ablaze.
Polish resistance fighters gave what
support they could. A few Jews

crawled out through sewers to
carry struggle on. The only possible
words are modest. And very quiet.

huge hardship   *will anyone come*

6. Theseus at Colonus

'Sometimes, no going forward
or back. All that can be done is wait.
Through waiting, one of several

ways may call – which to choose,
which to be chosen by. Then, no
return, for even going back is

a way forward, and coming
or going amount to the same thing.
It's all relative, depending where

and who you are, as the Chorus
will later remind us. So, Oedipus,
old friend, farewell. Long ago

at those crossroads, you made
your choices, and have attained
at last a little understanding.

See where, in peace, the Under-
world's Queen and Hermes lead
him gently, sightless, away.'

---

coming back, achievement   *favourable to see a great person*

(40)

Relieving, Releasing

rain   *under thunder*

Relief

Air thickened, pressed
in. Foreheads and temples
throbbed. Arms hung

listless, hands gummed
to sides. Sweat trickled
down skins. Then

under thunder, clouds
massed, rolled, broke. Rain
lashed and slashed soil,

rivers burst, mists rose,
fields lay soaked. As things
dried, scents of growing

plants rose up and
poured off everything.
On loosened breeze

we heard the swishing
and creaking of roots
deepening, sprouting.

rolling thunder   *heavy rain*

1. Graduating

She stands waiting in
a long line of students
in a vast auditorium.

She wears a hired blue
hooded graduate gown
and mortar board.

Her name is called.
She walks up six steps
on stage, then shakes

hands with a grinning
Vice-Chancellor, receives
a document stating she

has passed through and
out, and steps down on
the far side. A moment

poised between two
sets of steps. An entrance
and an exit. What next?

2. Pierce like a laser

Three hoodlum-brothers took
over. They all but ran City Hall. So
we appointed a new police chief.

He probed defences, infiltrated
ranks, clobbered small-timers, drew
out dupes, tricked key-players

to grass and double-cross. He
pierced like a laser, like a lightning
dart. He cornered and caught

all three – and got convictions.
A puritannical man, who set high
standards, a predator, intuitive

enough to read hoodlums'
minds, working in semi-dark,
unafraid of his own shadow.

A man like that, understanding
danger's character, is bound to
hunt down what lies hidden.

catching three foxes   *with a golden arrow*

3. Nat's chip

Nat gets chauffeured around in
a big shiny car. Lives in a mansion.
Aims to come across as chip-

off-old-block. But Nat's chip is
glued to his shouder. Craves kow-
towing, badgers allies, bullies

employees, swanks wealth,
loves reminding everyone how
loaded he is. Haughty, this

lout of scant honour earns
profuse honours. Cunning, sharp,
pernickity, wary, Nat praises

only those like himself who
need to get *very* rich, though
he'll ruthlessly pull down

whoever dares compete with
him. Chafing eyes clarify how
mean, perfidious, his spirit.

---

carrying heavy baggage *tempting thieves and robbers*

4. One big toe

Good idea to leave off
hanging out with sluttish
slovenly mates and give

up boozing, smoking and
getting stoned with them.
To breathe more air into

sluggish lungs. It's as if
one big toe had got caught
in a rat-trap. Not hard to

wriggle out, by moving
a bit, adjusting rhythm and
habit, doing without

unneeded luxuries such
as style, image, persona,
ornament, decoration,

superstructure, expect-
ation, and self's investment
in prefabricated formulas.

downsizing   *laying off*

5. Relief, release

It takes a person of
singular honour and integrity
to achieve relief and

release for others.
Petty-minded people may not
follow how this works in

practice but, unless
malicious, usually recognise,
even if only intuitively,

why and how they need to
be involved, each in his/her
own way. Therefore they

harbour no resentment
if one independent person
with honest motives

garners and modulates
support, releases people from
troubles, dispels danger.

a genuinely good person   *can relieve hardship*

6. In his penthouse suite

Occupying an entire floor atop
Viale Centenniale, Antonino's plush
penthouse overlooks slickest

downtown blocks. Amid hench-
men, minders, plus loyal gaggles
of paid and unpaid whores,

Tonino and his *consigliere* conspire,
plan, plot. They call him *Il Falcone*,
as he likes to hover and swoop.

At a darkened window opposite,
crouches Bobo Cappuccio, awaiting
Tonino's stroll on his *terrazza*.

Bobo couches a 5.56 mm. automatic
fitted with magnum universal nightsight
At 12:37 a.m., Tonino complies. Alert

from desert training, Bobo fires once,
hits his mark's third eye, and temporarily
frees streets from hoodlum bondage.

---

shooting a hawk   *perched on a high rooftop*

(41)

Decreasing, Shrinking

---

lake   *shadowed by mountain*

At the mountain's foot

In offices small
machines blink at one
another endlessly.

A rubber plant in
a window carries the
torch for our future.

Bees walk across
glass panes in search of
gone domains of nectar.

Scrunched plastic
bottles decorate paths
with reflections.

Walk not on stone
but foam and let it
rest your poor feet.

Hydrocephalous
chrysanthemums
bud and open.

---

tighten belt, resist disappointment   control anger, rein in desire

1. Losing perfection

I lose perfection, more
and more. And am glad
of that, wanting

less and less. Who isn't
vessel for perfection's loss,
gain, loss, gain, loss?

Whether gladness be
gain or loss, I'll be glad
to lose gladness too.

So do I teach myself
to abandon 'I', for this
will surely be done,

whose core is nothing
or less, whose being is
a not, knot, net, nest

of dust, water, flame,
light. Light my way, then,
of and to nothing.

2. Before you go

What though you
shrink? Soon you'll be
nothing anyway so

it won't hurt to slim
down. Drop a bit of
weight and baggage,

lose a few things,
have more of things less.
Lithe, lean, you'll

live longer. Better
supple, weak, like a
child, not brittle,

stiff. Hands, head,
belly, heart, in fluent
rapport. Alors

Travaillez. РАДИТЕ.
Arbeiten Sie. Lavorate.
Δουλέβετε. Gōng. 工.

---

diminishing self   无为   *freeing scope*

3. Clothèd all in green-o

A mountain looms over
a lake. On shore, between,
them, walk three men.

One leaves for a faraway
land. *Three, three, the rivals.*
Scouring wooded hills

around, the remaining
two find oak, ash, birch,
beech, willow and

poplar. They build
a trellis, winding, binding it
over and around, with

wattle, twigs, leaves,
until it stands, sound, as
a shelter. By a lake

under a mountain
when a man walks alone
he may find a friend.

three together   *lose one, find a companion*

4. To allow change

We didn't need
to set out to change
that much, only

to allow change
to happen. For we who
had built fine and

far on dreams had
forgotten they had died
in us. Still, we went on

designing ever higher
platforms for ambitions,
as we sculpted hopes

to fit each floor,
yet refused to admit
death's breath

(i. e. want of breath)
growing glowing blowing
around, in, through us.

---

decrease   *ailments*

5. *C'est la vie, mort de la Mort!*

One September Sunday
evening I walked out and
saw a zinc-and-nickel

half-moon in cloudless
sky above Cambridge, and
beside her, joined

in hinted outline, her
other half. And that was very
fine above my town's

trees and buildings. And
around 2 a. m. that night I
read Cesar Vallejo's line

Calor, Paris, Otoño, !cuanto estío
(Heat, Paris, autumn, so much summer) –
and then turned pages and read

C'est la vie, mort de la Mort! –
and that was even finer than fine.
Poetry is a criticism of death.

---

a tortoise   *worth ten pairs of shells*

6. The complete art of drowning

Being 2½ years old
this child falls, every
day she wakes, into

the lake of language.
Sometimes I watch her
from under this water

I swim my life through
having drowned here long ago.
Each day she gets better

at diving. Already she frog-
paddles on the surface. Her
gills are growing, lungs

disappearing. Soon
she'll learn the complete
art of drowning.

When engulfed in words
what worlds will she lose
and what world gain?

decrease or increase   *what do I know*

(42)

Increasing

---

wind above   *thunder below*

Sloop-building

Ballasted angled keels,
hewed smooth-curved hulls to
sit stable in water, caulked

carvel planks, lengthened
bowsprits, hoisted masts further
forward, slung neat jibs,

streamlined rudders, sewed
sails poised to hollow, billow,
wax, control – to follow,

caring and careful, all
winds' qualities. Our sloops
moved swift and cool in

elegance, now as swans,
now as dipping swallows. To
increase what's lower and

decrease what's higher
yields balance, depth, buoyancy,
almost-not-quite in surplus.

good to go somewhere   *favourable to cross great waters*

1. Spring wind

Unfazed by
current swerves
in temperature,

as if unbolted by a
troll from some huge
cave, spring wind

roars down our street
and everything that was
quiet is caught up

in thunder. So
where d'you think
you're heading

bolstered on this
invisible whish and rush
of insistent air, you

bursting word-shoots
out of silence's green
and pleasant ground?

2. *Del libro de la naturaleza*

He crowned my
three tongues of trees
with his ace of stars.

My four dusts
of meteor capped
his cask of sand.

My pack collapsed
in the teeth of his pair
of snow-white foxes.

I riposted with
a straight run of silver-
back eagle-drums.

He grinned and from
his left sleeve, pinkly,
pulled four winds.

I resurrected my
chances with five
gongs of cloud.

---

a tortoise worth ten pairs of shells   *can scarcely be refused*

3. Ambassador

Famine followed flood and
crops were ruined. She had not
asked to be ambassador

for her country, especially
one whose demeanour needed
modelling on that of an

immaculately courteous
and dignified beggar – not
fawning, and with no hint

of melodrama or self-
pity. Carrying out her duties
in a matter-of-fact style

that seemed to embody an
entire absence of stylishness
and so to deny style itself

she raised funds for invest-
ment, brought in new techno-
logy, created employment.

increase modesty   *from extremity, increase*

4. All I could ever

Getting old brings
not sadness and regret
but more hunger for

more life, more
energy, more desire
for doing, making

more – more of *now*,
more worlds. Walking
diagonally across

Petersfield from East
Road to Mill Road today
under an avenue of

Maytime beech trees,
each with its hundreds
of thousands of leaves

is all I could ever have
wanted, filled with all
time in the world

5. These poems shred themselves

These poems shred
themselves so fine they move
with consummate ease

between iron bars,
grooved slits in shutters,
cracks in plaster, vents

in sorrow, creases
carved within wind, and
slippages and knots in

time. So think nothing
of soundproof bunkers or
steel-clad tunnels. These

poems penetrate all
time's uniform chances,
fonts, chancels, right

across the Death that
will beat us hollow, take us
all out. But not *these*. Ha!

wind fair   *outcome good*

6. Leanne

Leanne brings benefit
to nobody else. She self-seeks
with hands, heart and mind

never fixed on anything but
insatiable desire for desire for
desire, and so on and on.

Nobody else can or will
satisfy her. When she sings
nobody else will join in.

Her words go round and
round in rings of self-service.
Many who now detest her

if included could easily
have been won over by her
brilliant enterprises. It'll

be no shock when she
gets struck at, struck off,
struck out, struck down.

(43)

Breaking through

---

clouds   *covering heaven*

Rainbow country

Black cloud blankets sky,
air thickens in storm, rain
pelts down – and see now

a rainbow! Just as this
decisive sweeping loosens
blocked streams,

empties drains, purges
standing ponds, and cool
blue penetrates this

land's farthest corners,
may this strike of ours
uproot graft, wash off

fear, clear corruption.
But until we have passed
fairer, better laws, let no

revenge or rancour rule,
although punishments be
swift, clean as this storm.

1. Strengths

Time to build strengths
anew. To grow them gradually,
soles-of-feet upwards. Begin

standing barefoot, legs
apart, knees bent. Next, explore
ground contact. Focus first

on heels, soles, balls of
both feet. Then on ten toes
one by one. Now imagine

a sapling in a garden
rooting through fertile soil,
meristems slow-probing

into earth's crust, coiling,
twisting, seeking each cranny –
until you're an unshakeable

tree, many-branched,
bending in winds, ready for
tempests, refuge for birds.

strengthening   *first the ten toes*

2. Flood-time

Our river has marooned us.
Tides of dark brown sludge
drift over this city, slicing

and stabbing, marking out
new islands. These shadows
adrift in sodden streets –

are they living or dead, or
neither one nor the other?
Our world seems fuller

than ever of non-human
controllers. Myths return
with new faces, new

names, unrecognisable.
With no treasures to store in
our homes, and chattels

worth next to nothing,
we'll be forced to move
onto higher ground.

---

shouts and shots late at night   *armed gangs on the prowl*

3. Abdullah's father

Abdullah's father was driving
when a sniper on the guardians'
side shot his young son

sitting in the back. He
whirligigged his car somehow
to hospital and carried his

boy in, blood-bathed. But
they couldn't save Abdullah.
So his father made enquiries

to join the rebels, militants,
resistance fighters, insurgents,
jihadis – call them what you

will – martyrs, terrorists,
heroes, human bombs. Before
detonating the explosive belt

wrapped around his waist in
the *souk*, killing twenty-seven
people, he made a video.

---

caught in hail   *maddened in misfortune*

4. Heroes, heroines

Shall they be forgiven, mur-
derous revolutionaries who *knew*
they'd change the world – yet

perpetrated atrocities? And
what of those worshippers of
far-flung beauty, steel-eyed

in their doing, whose grasp on
unyielding convictions crushed
foes and companions alike?

How mourn those proclaimed
and self-proclaimed heroes and
heroines who, possessed by

childlike angelic visions of
their own inflated importance
and genius, lacked one iota

of modesty or compassion?
Without fuss or compunction,
let's tear their statues down.

their words and actions   *no longer believed*

5. Mist dispersing

Meanings gather, adhere,
cohere. Those cunning eroders –
who ran and ruined our city

and confused its ministries
and academies by trouncing
sense out of words and

wheedling purpose from
thought – have gone suddenly
quiet. They'll be back soon

enough, claiming they're
something else now, something
fine, new, deserving

of our trust again. They
aren't to be believed now
any more or less than

before. Time to move
on past them, as if they
were mist dispersing.

6. In black snow

How many more of
them out there in black
snow, slithering on it,

trying to get back in,
beggars belief. Listen
to them outside our

window, scraping
nails of bony fingers
useless against solid

glass, whining in
slow wave-like mode
as if singing well-

rehearsed dirges,
mouth-corners drooling.
Are windows closed?

Are doors sealed?
Is our roof-dormer
bolted down?

---

howling, howling   *but no response*

(44)

Coupling

Fabric of the human orgasm

Entire fabric
of the human orgasm
meshed of timeless

space and light,
sunsets plashing
on wind-ravaged

waves, skydomes
dissolving, recongealing
and dissolving a-

gain into sleep,
dawns reconfirming
and rebrightening

everything – you I
am I you is – calm
unerring itinerant

relevant reverent
voice of the fourth
person singular.

1. Her white small-petalled voice

Her silk-lined voice
draped silence in falling
folds. Her flower-

scented voice soaked
all of him in longing. Her
white small-petalled cries

shimmered around his
thrusts, then bloomed and
exploded as sky dust.

Her dusky-petalled voice
shook out, fluttered wings
then sailed away endlessly

as he panted among her
unreachable borders. His
parched threadbare voice

lay patched with rain-
bows of hers as, lost and
found, they quietened.

---

tied down   *by the power of the receptive*

2. How amazing she was

How amazing she was
in that black sleeved dress,
pale skinned,

was it forty, or more, years
ago – and suddenly, now, for
no reason he can tell

except that he is getting
old, she touches his
memory with her glance,

her jaunty step past
then back towards him, her
full scent, her throaty

laugh, her deep voice,
soft mouth, measured words
and her ever quick

delightful mind, leaving
him gasping with
impossible longing.

fish in willow basket   *good the guests have gone*

3. Danitsa

Silver earrings she wore
inset with pearl and opal. And
that is how I remember her.

And that is all she wore
as she opened her arms and I
rose and fell inside her.

She was ocean
and archipelago. And she
was wave upon wave

and time a sheet rippling
loose on our unmade bed
while balcony doors

clattered and sea wind
hollowed and ballooned
through net curtains

and across night out-
side in unison cicadas
humbled the whole sky.

wearing out   _thighs and knees_

4. At least one of the liars

At least one
of the liars has
gone back to her

own homestead
on the other
side of Paradise

Island. For the time
being at least
we are free

from her malice
rippling and rocking
the foundations

of our trust, but
not for long. Be
aware she'll return

in the guise of
a cute sincere
spontaneous friend.

no fish in the kitchen   *and not for guests such as these*

5. Conspiring to live

After her father's
death and funeral,
a small glimpse

of happiness, or
rather, of its possibility,
occurred without

their realising it.
All evening they
talked ordinarily

and planned what
they'd do next. Then
they went to bed

and made love,
first tenderly, then
wildly, devouring

each other. Then
hugging and snuggling
went on talking.

gourd wrapped in pliant willow   *and meteorites from heaven*

6. In a green country

Old man stretched
on grass, gazing at
cloud-patched sky

in a green country,
thinks not of nothing,
not of anything.

Sun on forehead, then
quiet shade. A huge wind
gusts time away

through red
beech leaves that
sweep and dust

music across
August sky. Summer's
nearly over – and that's

fine. It's not time
itself but *his* time
tearing its heart out.

(45)

Massing

Midsummer Fair

Roll up for the Summer Solstice
and our huge fair on Midsummer
Common. Roll up for dodgems,

swings, merry-go-rounds,
spinning top, Big Wheel, helter-
skelter, rifle range, ghost train,

bucket-raffle, coconut shies,
penny-roll, hoop-la, whack-hammer,
flea circus, punch-and-judy,

face-painting, paint-slinging,
stilt-clowns, candy floss, toffee apples,
lollipops, sherbet, turkish delight,

nougat and peppermint rock. Plus
rattlers, roarers, hooters, pea-shooters,
balloons, goldfish. And the Fat

Lady. She reads palms. She'll
give you a purple heather sprig. She'll
grant you one single special wish.

1. See, one by one they arrive

See, one by one they
arrive, slowly they join in
as if gathering

ready for migration.
Your time has come too.
Their call calls you.

You too must rise up
now. Your only choice is
go with them. Steer

your communal course
by the magnetic poles, the
star-clock by night

and by cloudless
day, the sun's arc, angled
against horizons.

Now is your time for
following, not striking
out alone.

massing together   *go forward with them*

2. Small offerings

We've brought along
our small offerings, every
one of which we hope

will be included, used.
We've laid them out in
rows on trestle-tables

in our white-tiled white-
washed town hall. These
will go to children,

those to hospitals,
those to mine-workers,
and so on. Outside

the front gates, haggling
street vendors mingle with
beggars. Old ones cough,

huddle, kneel, squat, stroll.
Younger, fitter ones forage
in green plastic trash bins.

---

massing together   *bringing small offerings*

3. Julie

When her parents split and her
mother moved to a job in a town
down south, Julie was half way

through secondary school, so
she joined her new school half
way through her third year, at

precisely the age when English
teenage girls bond in exclusive
friendships. Few of her new

classmates had time or space
for her. Introspective anyway, she
grew resistant even to slight

advances from other girls, more
taciturn, morose, aloof. Trapped
in lonely inadequacy, feeling

snubbed, ostracised, lost, she
spent six months friendless, till
she started going out with boys.

---

hard to break in   *but a breeze blows above*

4. Beautiful September morning

Beautiful September
morning. I open my eyes
and then our curtains

and windows. Behind
the telegraph pole outside
this house, our rowan

tree's berries redden.
Men in shirtsleeves and
women with bare arms

walk or cycle to work.
Against the green wall of
number 72 opposite,

sun shadows patterns
of chimneys and sloping
roofs. Things of their

own accord fit and
cohere, including our
breaths and this air.

---

coming togewher   *in great good fortune*

5. Simon

Seemingly possessed by little
selfishness, Simon has brought
his party together with no clear

signs of his head being clogged
by unexplored shadows lurking
beneath his mind's surface,

waiting to be released and
realised in vile or violent action.
His speech? Courteous,

considerate. He comes
across as reassuring, modulated,
intelligent. From eyes, mouth,

and voice-timbre, it seems
he isn't lying. Rare qualities in
leaders these days. *Or is he?*

Who can be sure? Consider
what crazed megalomaniacs we've
suffered in living memory.

bringing people together   *is he to be trusted*

6. Celebrity

Samantha no longer feels
safe at the top. Now people
regard her royally. They

bow, curtsy, scrape,
stare, keep discreet distance.
Abandoned by gifts she

once had of inspiring
all those around her with
courage, smiles, devotion,

she no longer knows any-
body who might not abuse
her trust or take advantage

of her. Confiding now
in nobody, not even her
husband, and afraid to

leave her house, she
blames fate, curses fortune,
weeps innerly, alone.

(46)

Climbing

---

roots in the soil   *wood beneath earth*

Early morning

Dawn's rags hung
on a line of cloud.
Lightpods burst.

Every window
grew pearls. A
ship entering

harbour hooted
once through
haze below.

Our cockerel
responded
unstoppably.

A lone butterfly
skimmed
the sill. Behind

our rented
house the very
hills creaked.

1. Roots, roofs, routes

Purpose
differentiates life
from non-life.

In the depths of
the now, inexorably
we model futures.

Organisation
characteristic of life
is end-developed.

Wood has purpose
to grow through trees
root   leaf   seed.

The central nervous
system – most evolved of
teleonomic structures.

Whose purpose prompts
this? Is it we who pattern
language? Or does it us?

2. Lungfish

When cracks appeared
in the coastline of Pangaea,
spawning rivers,

lungfish, equipoised
on pectoral and pelvic fins,
balanced on caudal

rudder, slithered from
Panthalassa out on primeval
slime, then stumbling

higher, crawled up on land.
How many small steps then
to turtles, lizards, frogs?

With mobile pupils
in blurry eyes, did lungfish
track sun, moon, stars?

Without lungfish
no sighting of galaxies,
no dice, no poems.

3. Ghost town

We dispatched scouts
to spy out what defences
the people of the place

kept and commanded.
Quickly our runners came
back. Nobody, they said,

not even a dog. We can
take it any time. Whether
this was a trap or

diversion designed
to dissipate our energies
and give them the edge

who could tell until
later? Since no clues
stared us in the face

we checked charts,
tracked auguries, cast
stalks. And entered.

upwards into a ghost town   *no reason to hold back*

4. To protect the kingdom

'Hold this hand-sized oval
of wave-smoothed nephrite.
Pale-green, it once flaked

from cliff over our eastern
ocean. Now, take it, this water-
polished stone, to our western

border's highest passes.
There, scale the tallest peak
and at its top, build a pile,

immovable, of tapered slabs.
Then bury this milky jade deep
in that cairn's covered core.

Sacrifice no animals. Let
no person know such a piece
of perfection, delivered from

our kingdom's crown, stands
to mark our border, let alone
prise open its stony lock.'

---

presenting his offering of jade   *to the western mountain*

5. This now

Human speech first
surfaces on babble, spume
of oceanic language.

On delicate scales
phonemes balance speech-
sounds' distinctions.

Speaking's quick
joys arise, pointing,
naming this now.

Writing covers speech
over time, condensed in
points and lines.

Digit and word,
framing perfection,
treat time as field.

Poetry, inner speech
transformed, actually
opens this now.

6. Wall

We built the wall to keep
marauders and spies out
and our own peasants in.

Gates we manned with
high-trained élite guards,
never local conscripts.

But we needed markets.
And love and war like water flow
unnoticed in quiet places.

Border officials' sons
longed to escort far-travelling
merchants. Daughters

dreamed of wedding horsemen.
Over centuries, empire expanded.
Its frontiers shifted. Our wall

fell into disrepair. Stretches
still stand across our highest
hills and mountains.

(47)

Exhausting

lake   *drained of water*

We thirst but drink too little water

All joy
has dried up.
Nothing of love

we shared once
flows any longer be-
tween, among us.

We, both, all,
suffer exhaustion,
no-one listens

to anyone else's
deepest and most
heartfelt words.

Nobody looks
in anybody else's
eyes longer than

a mere flicker.
Accidental touch
is electric shock.

---

dried out   *worn, weary*

1. Monkey house

In the prison
called home, wife
and husband are

impossible cell-mates.
When guests arrive,
come on, roll up,

for a good peep
at life behind bars.
Now you are in

the monkey house,
and the animals
themselves, ourselves.

See, these my fleas
and these my jaws
and these my teeth.

Guests, this is small stuff.
Next we'll escort you to
the wild cat enclosures.

rump on a wizened tree stump   *staring into a gloomy valley*

2. Stalemate

Our sins catch
up with us
later, wearing

strangers' faces
armed in the very
latest judgements.

They steal up on us, un-
expected, slanted, askance,
coolly stabbing.

So these dead
straight eye-arrows
we each bore silent

through the nightmare
of our days together
were worn before

us by other
blurred unfamiliar
lingering shadows.

---

stale   *gutted, sickened*

3. Shadowland

Dear hope, may
we beg your pardon
for being, breathing

and bitter bereavement.
Ach, it is all
loss after loss,

and again and again
we stand to fall
to stand again till

when we sweat alone
and shiver out
our naked nights,

hordes of poisonous
clinging, blurred
unfamiliar shadows

reduce what we thought
durable strengths
to bitter jelly.

4. Readying, steadying

When all routes
lead back to this
present impasse

what use scheming
wishing dreaming
against this seeming

ice block steeping
the heart? Best
to read, walk

a little, meditate,
exercise – breathe in this
present, for there

is no other – keep
body and mind clear as
'one' can, say little,

be cheerful or at
least act it, be ready
for anything.

what gift   *in a gloomy valley*

5. Poisoner

I stepped across
the poisoner mixing
his cup for me

but, being stronger
forced him to the ground
and made him drink

his own concoction
in my place. And so
took him off out

of this life before
he could even say
sorry nicely or

farewell to what
or whoever here he
might have loved

even as you
yourself or I
myself love.

6. In two places at once

I lie on summer grass
in the park. Pigeon wings
flap air above me.

Willow under
wall is dying. I thirst but
drink too little water.

The man in red
knocks at my door. I'm not
in and he won't wait.

His letter sits on my
doormat. It says my account
is overdrawn. Time to get

on with things – read
symptoms, comprehend causes,
quietly pull in my belt.

A blackbird lands
close by. It hops towards me
cocking its head.

(48)

Welling, Replenishing

water

over wood

Consultation of the diagrams

Consultation
of the diagrams
is helpful

in the construction
of hypotheses, buildings
and voyages,

in the precise
locating of wells, mines,
bridges, towers, mirrors,

in alleviating
insomnia and fears
of death,

in the correct
turning of antennae
towards origins

and in all forms of
measurement and modes
of harmonising.

self-replenishing   *inexhaustible*

1. Who drinks from an old well?

Our well has dried
up. Not even birds
circle or settle here.

Our clerks have been
corrupted by one regime
after another. Even

lawyers and judges
have sold out. Kept in
pay of ministers

and landlords, they
collude in repression
and persecution.

Young and old alike
abandon houses, pack
bags, emigrate. Can

we find a dowser
with forked hazel
or willow branch?

buckets come up empty   *or half full of sediment*

2. Sometimes they answer

Sometimes they answer
even though I've asked
no question.

Sometimes they say
nothing, and appear to
smile and look away.

Or else they stare, like
the dead, through me
towards infallible sky

as quietly they pick
out question *behind*
question, before even

any thought lurking under
images and their nuances
or timbres has arisen

let alone right words
to articulate thought have
discovered me and opened.

3. From underground streams

We clambered down ladders
and ropes. Workmates at the
top let down shovels, sieves,

buckets, poles, mallets.
We dredged up a mountain
of mud and waste fallen

in and mulched down
there over years. Hauled out
rich stinking vegetable stuff

and rotten wood. Separated
it from clay to fertilise fields.
Hammered in new

stepping brackets and
handles as we relined walls.
Deepened and widened

entire cavity to hold more
water pooled from underground
streams than ever before.

4. *I Ching*

Fifty years my
friend, companion
and spirit-guide

always trustworthy,
never diffident
never irrelevant

solid yet flowing
firm yet yielding
radiating images

self-replenishing
inexhaustible
fathomless

ever-fresh well –
in plumbing you
I soar

feet still
grounded rooted
in *this here now*.

5. I lower my question

I lower my
question on a rope
of thought.

I draw up
water-wisdom. It
flows everywhere.

I drink from a fund
of deep light. Could
wine be sweeter?

If its taste is bitter
then I swallow it. Its
bitterness is me.

Is it sweet? Then
I'm thankful – but
keep aloof from

drugs coiled in
sweetness. These ways
I come and go.

6. Well, inexhaustible

Self-replenishing
and inexhaustible
well, generous

secret, open face
of Underworld, with
rounded mouth

and level gaze –
polished mirror and
porthole of night,

silvery cord
and vertical pipe
invisibly joining

heaven and earth's
skin and core,
beneath these eyes

in your reflection
on the sky's forehead –
a star.

(49)

Shedding

---

fire   *burning under water*

Revolutionary Cadre

Our self-appointed task
questioning, challenging myths,
based on our own longing

to see them tumble,
collapse, crumble, wither away –
towers of bricks brought

down by us – and what
pleasure to see this happen
before our very own eyes.

This, we dubbed Dialectic.
Our dreams? We invested them
in debunking, interrupting,

clashing. Why? Not to
put up with the blur and glaze
of half-truth? Although

catastrophe beckons us
repeatedly, we remain
a reservoir untapped.

1. The statues

One night the statues
in our parks and squares
climbed down from

their pedestals, tore down
four trees (oak, elm, poplar,
birch), stripped off leaves,

sawed off branches, then
ferried trunks to the museum
for battering rams,

broke down its doors
and liberated fellow statues.
Venus smashed a truck.

A headless Winged Victory
lifted a tram, toppled it and
crushed nine passengers.

Poseidon flooded the reservoir.
Three of the Burghers of Calais
set fire to the Town Hall.

2. Increasing light

Increasing light we did think
possible, and worthy as goal.
Therefore we calculated

strategic phased attacks
on choicest targets, first on
provincial towns, those

most vulnerable, taking on
scant risk of loss, expense or
pain borne by ourselves,

then cities increasingly
powerful and established,
until, well-practised, we

stood ready to challenge
Central Authority, besiege its
cabals and fortresses, take

over and reconstruct
the entire state edifice, its
baggage and apparatus.

---

day of action   *what is the right time*

3. Making mistakes and enemies

In making mistakes
and enemies, we did not
do so languidly, but

deliberately and un-
hesitatingly cut competitors
and opponents down.

So we destroyed many
we still loved or once had
loved and many more we

didn't give a damn about
who happened to occupy
any position blocking

our road to our goal – *the*
Road and *the* Goal. Those
we wiped out included

unwary, innocent and
ignorant passengers. We got
good at creating victims.

declaring abolition   *the people's army takes charge*

4. While we suffered losses

While we suffered
losses keenly, believing
ourselves sole

light spreaders, we
claimed and continued
to claim for ourselves

purity, clarity, honesty,
cunningly purloining from
general availability all

aspects and facets of
those particular virtues
(could they have been

other than virtues?) for
our own convenience and
use. Doing none of this

wittingly, in light's name
at times spreading dark,
we built on destruction.

5. Shedding

Before Xiao Yao
effected changes in the world,
in others, he changed

himself. He went down
into darkness and silence,
where he shedded *things*,

spacetime, life-and-death,
even his own breath. Then
from that core that is

nothing and everything,
a fire inexhaustible flowed
in streams through and

along his fingers, to and
into whatever he touched.
Were you, who were

lucky enough to meet
him, charged through
his charge? Changed?

tyger tyger   *burning bright*

6. 'Like dew upon the morning'

Some old Fascists have
died. A few still behind bars
are likely to get out soon.

Most have faded away
'like dew upon the morning' –
in their own eyes, heroes

in battalions of the brave,
patriot-honour-defenders,
ever secretly unrepentant

believers in values they
first fought for, now taboo.
Entirely harmless? Maybe.

Pot bellied, varicose-veined,
frequently pissing old geezers
with enlarged prostates –

typical old men. Some wish
they'd died young. Many have
sons, waiting for revenge.

---

some day   *will they stage a comeback*

(50)

Cooking, Sacrificing

---

fire

over wind and wood

Cauldron

One world, one entire
being. Full humanness,
highest fullness –

    Here is the cauldron
    with lid of beaten bronze
    and two ear-handles.

Honesty, grace,
magnanimity. The leaf dies
and forgives the tree.

    Here is the cauldron,
    its three bronze feet
    shaped lions' paws.

Justice and love, pour
both in the brew. These
the meanings of sacrifice.

    Carry the cauldron
    with a jade-inlaid rod
    through its handles.

a vessel for cooking   *and sacrifice*

1. Croesus, Lord of Lydia

Croesus, Lord of Lydia,
soliciting divine *Sicherheit* to
underwrite his half-baked

war plans against Persia, paces
nights through his Sardis palace
and devises a plan – to test

the seven wisest of the wise
in the known world. To each
he will send an ambassador

charged with the same brief. On
the hundredth day after departure
each is to ask the oracle what

he, Croesus, son of Alyattes,
is doing at that moment, where-
upon a scribe is to copy down

the Sybil's response and
the ambassador to return with it
post-haste, witnessed, sealed.

empty out   *the stale stuff*

2. Seven embassies set sail

One to the oasis-shrine of Amun,
Desert Lord of Good Counsel, Zeus
of Libyan Sands,

two to the trickling spring, sleep
sanctuary of Melampian Amphiaros
at Kalamos above Oropos,

third to Apollonian Abae in
Phocis, fourth to Thessalian Dodona
of oak-hung wind-gongs,

fifth to Branchidae in Milesia,
sixth to the Trophonian cave in
Boeotian Lebadoia (Levadhyá),

and seventh to snake-guarded
Delphi brooding on waves over
its gulf of wind-tossed oliviers.

Of all seven responses,
writes Herodotus, none but
the last has been recorded.

---

cautious   *about where to go*

3. Against Parnassian blue

The Delphi-bound embassy
disembarks at Itea, hires local
packmules and drivers,

trudges summer-silvered
slopes to bee-haunted honeyed
Apollonian Delphi, set

in its green and ochre bowl
against Parnassian blue. And
on the hundredth morning

they don white tunics and
set out tasteful gifts on trays
before the Pythoness –

all of which she ignores
and before the Lydian ambassador
can utter one obsequious

word, cuts to the chase
in her sing-song curving
accented dove-speech.

regret   _washes away_

4. What the Delphic Oracle said

I spy by butterfly. I dowse by bee
and I have filtered water's memory
to count for every droplet in the sea.

I sail disasters and ride distant storms
to track the links and paradoxal forms
reclusive among averages and norms.

My inner eyes read souls. My spirit-hands
finger sea-beds and unscroll distant lands
to calculate their particles of sands.

I coil hatched hurricanes in wax-sealed jars
and count on Chronos and his avatars
to read the rings and number of the stars.

I excavate gone dialects of bone
and know the thoughts forgotten men have thrown –
thinking themselves unheard – at rock and stone.

Your death's an empty window I've seen through.
I've walked out and surveyed the long dark view
as if it were an evening avenue.

---

5. A tortoise and a lamb

Croesus devises the most
improbable activity imaginable
for the oracles to scry. Carves

up a tortoise and a lamb. Then
boils their bits in a brass cauldron.
But Pythoness sings to his envoy

> *Hear now, clear as a bell*
> *what I see at this time. On*
> *my sense strikes the smell*
>
> *of stew, boiling over flame,*
> *a tortoise with broken shell*
> *mixed with flesh of lamb*
>
> *as high hand warranted.*
> *Bronze the cauldron's body,*
> *bronze the cauldron lid.*

So chants the priestess, triply
fooling Croesus. He makes sacrifices.
Wages war on Persia. Loses.

---

cauldron   *fine yellow ears, fine handle*

6. The foiler fooled

King Croesus, big-time
loser – the foiler fooled
or the fooler foiled?

Carry the cauldron
on a jade inlaid rod
passed through its handles

Beat the system and gods?
Defy Nature? Hoodwink Death?
They'll get you in the end.

Was the Graal a skull,
a jewel-inlaid chalice – or
jade-ringed cauldron?

Hitler Stalin Pol Pot
Amin Hussain Gadafy
Atishoo all fall down

A hollow sacrificial
vessel of hammered bronze
shouldered by two men.

---

sacrificial vessel   *rings of jade*

Shaking, Quaking

thunder   *on thunder*

Thunder rolling

No time, this, to retreat
to native village or valley,
self-buried in routine,

or behind habit-mask
in market, bar, tavern. No
place is safe or exempt.

Now calls you out. No
hiding, no delay. For now is
when action, swift, clear-

headed, decisive, must
move matters forward, il-
luminating all it touches

with hope, love, justice –
or rot will spread further.
So no sicklying over

this now with doubt's
pale cast. You're trained
to be ready for this.

1. Let her

Lord of eagle-watched
Olympus and Dodona
of ringing oak-gongs,

Perkunas king of storm-
battered forest, Perun of
iris-lake and moth grove,

Thor drummer
of glacier and ice-cap,
Donar river-cracker,

Indra delta-flooder,
Parjanya cloud-rider,
Baal filler of oasis

and desert drummer,
Yahweh scale-tuner of
lightning's ladders,

Aktsin the hammerer –
has she conceived our
first child?

thunder   *then laughing and talking*

2. Revolution

Fire-fights in our streets.
Bombs dropping. So – join
the rebels, no way back.

No choice. Each night,
more fighters creep like shadows
into our scrap-of-a-town. They

gather on corners in small
persistent groups. Never have
so many unknown faces

been seen here. Our women
and children have fled to camps
across the border. Nine days

it took them. Who knows if
they'll return. They may well
lose one another, and we

everything. But the old regime's
dictator has lost half his generals.
One by one they're defecting.

3. The storm's heart

Blackness reached
out into the storm's heart
and stabbed and pierced

through it. Bloody streaks
dripped, then poured over storm's
body, smothered, quelled,

until only rust and rust's
shadows covered earth and sky
in swirls of greys and ochres.

Muffled drumbeats melted
in echoes. On the other side
of that misted island behind

our mauve mountain, wave
crests clutched at pebbles with
foam-white fingers. Things

grew clearer, crisper, as if
opened by dawn. A pellucid
calm highlit everything.

4. Thunder

Thunder booms.
Storm blasts our town
to its roots. Our river

bursts its banks. Up-
rooted trees at perilous
angles half float, snag

debris. All bridges
are broken. Giant tides
batter our sea walls,

flood our harbours,
smash our buildings.
We've no defences.

We thought ourselves
strong, clever, secure.
Not any more.

Some haven't
survived. We don't yet
know how many.

5. Riots

Flak and disturbance
rumblings far and near –
down our road too,

rioting in a dozen cities
four days, five nights, in
twenty separate areas,

in the capital fires flaring,
shops looted, paving torn,
men, women, children

hurling stones, bricks,
bottles, in running battles,
whole streets cordoned

off by police. Whose
fault, this, who deserves
to be blamed, who

to be punished? Those
with little or nothing have
next to nothing to lose.

is it time yet   *to take decisive action*

6. In the storm's eye

We woke to a frantic rattling
of windows in grooves and sockets,
and slates, dislodged from roofs,

smashing onto pavements. Bins
and lids went clattering, Leaves, bags,
papers swirled. When we drew

curtains, expecting rain, cool
blueness ripped racing clouds. We've
gone round the whole house

packing vents, sealing cracks,
refastening bolts, to shut out
this crazed invader who has

laid siege to our world. But
muttering, creaking, swelling
in tune to fire engine sirens,

it's blacked out our sky. Holed
up, we joke, pretending this isn't
a thing we'd wish would end.

---

nearly through this time   *cautious next*

(52)

Stilling

---

mountains above   *mountains below*

He left his city

He left his city,
walked out past
wind-battered scanty

fields carved vertiginous
in terraces, sheds wedged
against hillside rills

nestling perilous on
edges and past these
higher still where

scant trees grew,
to a cloud-smothered
mist-wreathed hut

on a gorse-spattered
plateau. Friend, he said
on arrival, I bring you

no gift, either of inheritance
or of adequate skill. None
the less, here I am.

1. Meditation at Hourn Farm

Shi Jing leads us
in meditation. Three times
he rings his bowl-bell.

I settle slowly, mind
top-heavy turbulent giddied
not yet ready to look down

let alone gaze into deep
nothing. So I watch those
facing me. Shi Jing sits,

purple cloth draped on
left shoulder, slung over
back and left arm,

right hand resting palm
on knee, forefinger and
thumb touching. He

neither smiles nor frowns.
Between doing and undoing,
he sits in his white beard.

still   *at the toes*

2. Gatekeeper

Shi Jing's bowl-bell sits
beside him on its red and
yellow diamond-patterned

cushion. Bowl-bell does
nothing, has and knows no
desires, indulges no needs

or affections. Lacking
hope or desire, bowl-bell
has no views on things,

no opinions, options or
ideas, and sits or seems to
sit in perfect rounded

silence. Not focussed,
not inattentive, sturdy
bowl-bell remains

ever at-the-ready. When
merely tapped by striker
bowl-bell rrrrrrrings.

still at the heels   *calves fidgeting, stiff knee joints*

3. Approximations

One might say: bowl-bell
is a *wu wei* adept. One might
say: played, bowl-bell slices

into and through silence.
Or: bowl-bell stirs sound
into silence where both

mingle and dissolve in
(into) each other. Or: draws
sound across silence's cool

bridge/page/field/string.
Or: paints white silence (over)
with sound's eloquent

elegant strokes. And so on.
Nice ways of putting things?
Maybe – but inadequate.

Studying absolutely no-
thing, bowl-bell possesses
skills to open heart-gates.

---

still at the waist   无为   *heart overheats*

4. The ringing, *zhong,* the centre

Arrow-like bowl-bell
rings and hits each of us
in very *veryness.* Pierces

into heart of into
soul of into spirit of in
to core of of of our –

what? Mmm could
one say something like *isness*
(*izzness*) or *whatness? Zhong*

goes the arrow through
bull's eye of any-/every-
where-when, both

general and *this*-specific,
unerringly accurate and
utterly aimless, izzing

without intention. *Ping
Pling Ding Bing Ring Sing
Zing Qing Jing ZHONG*

---

5. Nothing happens

Don't expect anything
to happen, he said, before
entering meditation.

And nothing did. Or
rather, what happened
was precisely *nothing.*

Hm. Words don't work
very well at this because
it was outside language

even though a kind of
language of its own – one
I'm beginning to learn? –

a learning consisting
of unlearning. What happens
is nothing. Everything

fills to the brim with
absolute nothing. That's what
empties (into) everything.

---

still at his jaws   无为   *words ordered, regret disappears*

6. Ringing his bowl-bell

Shi Jing strikes his
bowl-bell with its mallet.
What did you hear?

he asks. I heard a bell
echoing, says one. A chime
ringing, ringing, ringing,

says another. And
another, a thread reeling
and unreeling through me.

Another, It woke me
up. And another, clever,
I heard the sound

of silence. Shi Jing
pauses. No, you didn't, he
says, What you heard

was (   ). Again he
touches his mallet to its
bowl-bell. We enter.

---

keeping still, honest　　　　　无为　　　　*sincerity won't leave him*

(53)

Shifting

---

trees   *on the mountain*

Mountain fir

Your arrow-summit pierces
starkest light silhouetted as
if against blue flame-heart

and stilled so transparent
on hill-height as to appear a pool
unrippled by wind, unmargined

but by world-edge. Then, your
lower trunk so thick-wrapped
in haze as to be visible only

as ghost-pillar, as figment
of itself. Then, deeper than nether
crawlings of ants and spiders

or glide of sleek-headed adder
among mosses, deeper than shadows
within shadow, coil your roots

beside inky Lethe around
whirlpooling cauldron of black
light, everything's mainstay.

---

on the mountains, trees   *slow they grow*

424

1. Wild geese

Slow   the wild
geese in V formation
approach the shore

Slow   the wild
geese land on the crag
settle high up

Slow   the wild
geese wing ways
to highlands

Slow   the wild
geese settle on
tree branches

Slow   the wild
geese arrive among
blue-grey hills

Slow   the wild
geese pace cloud-avenues
over mountains

---

slow the wild geese   *approach the shore*

2. River-run

Spring. Ice melts.
Capillary channels, meandering
rivulets, gather, merge, flow.

Minuscule moving molecules
among mountains meet and
mingle, filling, overfilling

in torrents surging down
gullies, tumbling through ravines,
cascading into valleys

to feed broad sluggish
jugular – river with marshy
backwaters dotted with

islands like horns, joined
by more and more tributaries,
bridged by splendid cities.

River, you've grown into
an empire of water, an avenue
colonising fish, birds, men.

slow the wild geese   *approach the high crag*

3. A challenge

To die of sickness isn't
inevitable. Why not instead
prepare for living well

until life's last moment
comes? And though sickness
in old age be expected

norm, why not step out
of such mind-habits, such
conditioned addictions?

Time to simplify and
purify things, eat less, even
cut out grains (hard),

drink water and teas,
walk, meditate, practise
taiqi, daiyin, qigong,

become more supple
in body and spirit, write
clearer, finer poems.

4. All the best books

All the best books say
you can't do it through books
You have to find a teacher.

Then you have to follow,
cultivate, practise daily. Years
he went looking. Several

proclaimed or self-proclaimed
Masters took him on. Their paths
turned away. Or he wasn't ready.

Others disappointed or
saw through him. Then looked
across him, far, way off.

He worked his own passage,
learned truths from friends and
companions, from other

creatures, nature, and dead
masters, whose words/deeds re-
corded in books outlive Death.

slow the wild geese   *descend onto trees*

5. What the tinker said (2)

The road ahead
swirls in and out
of rainbow

no path could
be more clear
way of sky

and way of stone
way of oak and way
of leaf, way

of river
and cloud, way
of swan and

snake, way of
tortoise and tiger
way of dragon

way of word
and not-word, way
of air and fire.

slow the wild geese   *approach the hills*

6. You, perfectly

I have foreseen
you reading this be-
fore you were ever

conceived. And
so for sure I recognise
you, perfectly. How

and how long this
lives depends now
and ever on you.

On the other side of
this page *I* lurk as well
behind your eyes.

Seek me nowhere.
Whoever or whatever I
was dissolves. All

that's left is this, in
your eyes, ears, mouth,
heart, mind, spirit.

slow the wild geese　　　　　　*approach the cloudy avenues*

(54)

Wooing, Courting

---

lake   *under thunder*

Push me, said the girl

Push me, said the girl,
into this and I shall run
away or cut my wrists.

I won't do it. This grotty
old fart with paunch and
stinking breath isn't for

me. I don't care about
his character, intentions or
wealth. His smiles hurt.

It's cook in his kitchen
I surely will be and prisoner
in his flatulent bed. But

what lies out there, far
apart from him, farther than
I can see, shimmering in

delight and danger
at dream-edges, calls me.
I've no choice but follow.

1. The widow of Stockport

The magistrate Parving-Potts
has just been widowed. He has
three young daughters.

Who will bring them up?
He longs for a son to inherit
and manage his estates.

The widow Eunice Biggs
from Stockport, Cheshire,
is not past-child-bearing.

Her dark eyes wide open,
her hips large and comfortable,
her breasts well-rounded.

Though she is of humble
background and her rough
speech betrays a vulgarity,

to her will fall the burden
of bearing and raising an heir.
Her stepdaughters detest her.

marrying   *his second wife*

2. Loyalties

Your sad keen eyes blared
you needed tenderness. From
him you got intelligence and

much good that did you
when he turned sardonic
and left you for a younger

far more self-seeking and
more muddled woman – who
in her turn, turned against

him. Abandoned by her,
he cracked. Then did you
turn effective mother

ready to minister unto
him, through his final cancer,
devoting to him all

your dark instinctive
tenderness, your dogged
keen invincible loyalty.

blind in one eye   *still able to see*

3. *Hoy le ha entrado una astilla*

Today a splinter has
got(ten) into her. A sallow
pillow is her flesh – and

her soul, still sallower
and hollower a pillar. No-
body can guess where

it lodges inside her or
how deep it has got(ten)
in, let alone what it is

made of. Admit, you
doubters, this splinter
does exist. Confess

she is sainted for the
rich injurious sting of it,
its harrowing of her,

for so she becometh
martyred as a sliver pure
past paradise portal.

here comes his second wife   *or is she his third*

4. Still guest and stranger

She is still guest and
stranger as she enters
nothing's premises.

Expectations and
promises she takes off
with shoes at the door.

Her heart that raced has
quietened. Happiness is not
in quest or question.

Head stilled and
tilted, in lowered
gaze she bows.

Her host welcomes her
into his house. She enters
the chamber of nothing.

The light in her head
turns around. She is part
of brightness streaming.

5. Animated, the daughters

The daughters must be
right. They absolutely will
not swallow their earlier

views, which were clearly
100% right then too, as they too
get swallowed by overriding

consequence. They wave
goodbyes as they compose
themselves. They get in-

to cars and blow kisses.
Bye-hye. Love you. See you
after whatever-the-event

may be. Soon times
of no-afters will come
and even the oldest

of old women turn
back into daughters, their
own goodbye-sayers.

her dress didn't look   as gorgeous as his second wife's outfit

6. Her sudden mood switches

Her sudden mood switches,
in his eyes for no apparent
reason, but always in hers

his fault, locked him out
of her bed and, eventually
numbed his mind when-

ever he was in the house
at the same time as her. So
if she was in he went out

and vice-versa. When her
complaints about him boiled,
she said he never saw her

for herself, only for what
he could get out of her or
use her for. And he never

took a blind bit of notice
of what she really was, felt,
thought, believed, wanted.

no fruit   *basket empty*

Abounding, Brimming

Things, brimming

Sunlight slanted
through the elders
and the rowans.

We wash things. We pour
oil on them. We use them
for carrying, cooking, cutting.

A solitary jogger
pounded down
the dawn.

Things wing through time
acquiring and discarding
meanings like feathers.

A splinter of
rainbow sat on
the horizon.

Things leap and fall in
note and value. Meanings slip
from one thing to another.

---

under sunlight   *among stars, at noon*

1. Adhering, inhering

The way the light
adheres and inheres
to or in things

as if glued or
as part of their
fabric, stuff,

very grain
and yet constant
in its changing

is surest gift
of world and time.
Whatever else

may go or come
this light changing
on surfaces

is delight, is
glory, the unique
common miracle.

2. What and all

This is what and
all there is, always
overspilling in

bounty yet rarely
enough. This walking
on miracle ground

this song of air
colours of morning
sky-dome

this I and
sense-of-I, of-me, this
sense-of-you with

actual you-there
you-here, you-everywhere
this last and first

unquenchable
desire, this constancy
of beautiful thirst.

3. Consoling, abundant, terrifying stars

Consoling, abundant,
terrifying stars, you humble
the identity of me to

a point less than zero,
to zero's irreducible core,
whatever such might be.

What an irrelevance
any such entity as 'I'
compared with your

high hushes and rushes
mastering unimaginable
time-space, vast zones

of your habitations.
Here, away from city glare
and faced with you and

my death, you squeeze
all identity out of me. And
that's fine, majesties.

4. What Zhang Zai said

Zhang Zai said, Earth is
a thing. Heaven is a marvel.
One look up at the stars

at night far from any city,
and what he meant is clear.
Yet since this world

floats on, in, across
and through heaven, doesn't
being in and on the world

mean being in and on heaven
too? And if so, don't seas, rocks,
soil, air contain as much

heaven as stars and
interstellar spaces up there?
Therefore, isn't heaven

as much in my fleshed
mortal hands and yours as
it might lurk in any god's?

---

among stars   *on the roof*

5. Heaven-stuff

The grandeur of
these infinite spaces
gives delight and

hurts not. Spaces,
comets, stars, galaxies,
quasars, supernovae

fold in, over and
upon themselves –
not silent but

dusty with music.
They stretch around,
among, within

us who, being
on earth, thereby
reside in heaven,

among heavens,
made of the same
heaven-stuff as they.

among stars   *on the floor*

445

6. What Zhang Zai knew

Heaven is more
than discernible sky.
You could never

see all of heaven
or even imagine it.
Zhang Zai knew

heaven is actually
where we are already –
fully empty and

emptily full,
unfathomable and
insubstantial, both

by substance and by
our irreducible material
sources and ends

in the way of ways.
Buoyed in void we
rise, fall, rise, fall.

(56)

Travelling

fire   *over the mountain*

Like starlings

Transparent and quick as
autumn wind is how you arrive,
October poems, after long

learned practice: of unlearning
and waiting, and following and
forgetting craft. Now on

your meaning-waves, words
surge, swarm, gather, split off
and re-form, like flocks

of assembling starlings
that come together of their
own cackling accord,

connected, wayward, mazy,
never touching in flight. Go
your winter ways, poems.

By February or March
you'll be eastbound again, for
Lithuania, Latvia, Estonia.

---

travellers   on speckled wings

1. Borderers

In those days, we
travelled light, took
few possessions.

Preferring tortuous
mountain passes to
trodden ways

across plain or by river
we spurned highroads
and marked frontiers.

Today we remain
borderers, go-betweens,
our languages always

dialects, our eyes wary
in half-light, attentive by
dark to seven senses,

our ears alert, taking
in more than ever our
bland expressions let on.

a curious attention   *to finicky detail*

2. Resident ghosts

We are the edge-folk,
the end-and-beginning
people, suspicious of

unstated intentions in
voice behind voice,
glance beneath glance,

word undeclared by
self-declared friend, charm
of hostess, tactic of proven

and trusted ally, agenda
of respected colleague,
motive of best-disposed

neighbour. Captains,
remember, we are called
on, called for, called

away, by resident ghosts
in your futures, and at all
times are ready to leave.

3. Auditors

Cunning in contest and
devious in battle, in some
things we never cheat, for

we are 'people of the book'
too. We keep our accounts
as carefully with the gods,

our gods, that is, as
with men. Auditors
of actual and impossible

numbers, peering in
sand grains, through
ashes, in dust, we scry

vaster darknesses
to sieve and track
from time's tendrils

minuscule miracles
and to map origins
and ends of light.

4. Now I confess

Now I confess, what
I want is nothing
other than this

small pack I carry
home this path that takes
me where I have to go

home itself being
the way itself
and path itself

path on the path
way on the way
way of sky and way of stone

way of oak and way of leaf
way of hammer and rainbows
way of air and fire

home this curious
journey full
of unexpected mornings.

---

lodging   道   *but not staying*

5. Elsewheres

Things have a habit
of accumulating elsewheres
or otherwise dissolving them.

Things accrue sediment
of memories. Then
they, or we, die.

But we, boarders,
borderers,
go hunting

an unnamed creature
that stands clear
from its surroundings

no matter where it finds
itself, in and among
things. We too prefer those

elsewheres. To run
with that creature
on a field of sky.

---

to shoot down   *an impossible bird*

6. Longing

Over the world, what
the songs sing of is
pain, lamentation, exile –

gust-blown travellers,
migrants in hope
all on the move

to and from different
zones, different voices,
the same song,

the same plangent
tone and expression,
the same yearning

for safe haven,
for a home familiar
in the quiet heart,

a single welcoming
face to greet the ex-
hausted traveller.

(57)

Blowing, Billowing

the wind   *on the wind*

What's that whirring

What's that whirring
in the guttering? Only
the wind muttering.

And that clattering
above the ceiling? Your spirit
staggering and reeling.

And that sighing in
the eaves? The gale that
frets and grieves.

And that rattling in
the chimney? The breath
of Death, your enemy.

And that whimpering
in the rafters? The wind's
weepings and laughters.

And that rattling in
the basement? Your soul
breaking its casement.

1. Father, counting

I heard you counting, said
the boy to his father, the woodcutter,
in the deep forest. What were

you counting so fast, so light?
Why, the whispers of the wind,
replied his father. And how

many were there? said the boy.
As many as corners in the forest,
forests in a moment, moments

in a wingbeat, wingbeats
in a smile, smiles in a daydream,
daydreams in a building,

buildings in a soul, souls in
a song, songs in a circle, circles in
a heart, and hearts in a whisper.

Those were the twelve I counted
so fast, so light, my son. And now,
you can count them with me.

whether forward or back　　　　　　　　*with a warrior's firmness*

2. *Hah!* replied the wind

This is being swept
home. So, thank you, wind.
I've no more arguments

with you. *Hah!* replied
the wind. Arguments are
bowls of questions mixed

with a deal of dust. Some
get cleaned up and cleared
and others spat out

and spilled. At the end
of every good argument
containing many

interesting matters, at
least one question always
gets left behind. This

book of yours may
be done. But this question
outlasts your book.

confused   *consulting too many experts*

3. Marcello

Compliant, acquiescent,
accommodating, Marcello smiled
and helped whenever asked.

Making small impressions,
upsetting nobody, he followed
instructions gladly, but never

led, from front or back,
or took difficult, dangerous,
or decisive initiatives. Like

a fluttering creature wafted
on every wind, he moved only
when prompted. Gradually

his winning smile twisted
and withered into obsequious
disappointment on a wry

embittered face. Downturned
creases around eyes and mouth
twitched and shrank in scowls.

---

wind-blown   *compliance, resentful*

4. Wild creatures

And although naming
was neither our prime desire
nor our special business

or even accidental or
acquired task or purpose
and while weather

like mood lay coiled
unpredictable, fluctuating
between extremes, still

beauty would shake out a
more than occasional dazzling
in incident, as accident —

glade, hill, mountain, valley,
badger, fox, hawthorn, bramble,
swan, archipelago, island —

so, as we travelled,
calling, we named names
and meant them.

---

hunting in woods   *catching then releasing wild creatures*

460

5. Wind's paths

The wind's paths
can't be written. Neither
ink nor blood will

code the wind.
Here is my home
inside the wind

and where I belong
in the wind's core.
Don't ask for me

in fields or houses,
on streets or mountains
or among companions.

Thanks to the wind
nothing I am
is usable. Indeed, I

am so changed by
the wind, soon I'll have
become invisible.

6. House, voice, leaf

This house
not mine, but
the wind's.

This house
stands against and
in the wind.

This house
a knife that
cuts the wind.

This voice
a knife that cuts
the wind in half.

Your voice
a knife that cuts
time in half.

Leaf, double
edged blade that
halves the wind.

(58)

Joying, Enjoying

lake   *over lake*

Two lakes, joined

Two lakes, joined,
one above the other
along the same river:

Upstream, the Derwent
and, below,
<u>the</u> Ladybower.

When two lakes join
together they
do not dry up.

One draws the other
through constant
self-replenishing.

Upstream, the Derwent
and, below
the Ladybower.

Joyousness:
two lakes, joined,
one above the other.

1. Lakeside

Away from that shoreline,
Aging man. Abandon
the swell on the tide

that has pulled you
many times leeward, to
hug familiar dangers

and cling to idiosyncrasies
of currents in recognised
channels. An offshore breeze

is tugging you to this lake's far
wilder side, where no youngsters
bathe naked or toddlers

paddle in inlets. That way, slow
and steady, you'll row her, your
companion, into mainstream

waters, masked only by
Coppice Island, which joins
your two lakes together.

2. Past Coppice Island

Once you've rowed past
Coppice Island, everything
you do and say can be (is)

lighter and cleaner than
wherever you've been or
have come from. You

can float your very
own waterscapes and even
invent geographies

just as here the words
go flowing on under
and around these oars

this poem-boat wields
as it takes us slow and
steady both together

to the point where it
comes ashore in an inlet
of a bay called silence

sincere   *regret disappearing*

3. Young Joline

Triply gifted in intelligence,
charm and beauty, she made
good headway by

smooching and smarming
up to bosses, colleagues, with
her open smiles, yeses

and gifts, including those
of her own body as occasional
pleasure vehicle or flag or

beacon. She lifted quite a few
of them up and quite enjoyed it
herself, which was OK while

it lasted. But when they dumped
her she felt as if marooned alone
miles from shore in a caïque

in the middle of some huge
lake, no sail or oars, black clouds
brooding, night coming on.

---

borne on flattery   *brings no fortune*

4. Young Jake

An unexpected inheritance
from an unknown benefactor
left young Jake vulnerable

and open to temptation.
Companions he trusted
were his seducers. Easy-

come-easy-go good-time
friends helped him spend a
good part of his fortune

without thought or self-
criticism. He enjoyed wasting
time and money hanging out

with them till, out of the
blue, a need to check bank
balance and conscience

struck him, spurring him
to change his life, choose new
directions, start working.

leaving off dark joys   *escaping the sickness unto death*

5. Young Jeanette

A twinge of danger
in the pleasure of being so
close to her commander

set young Jeanette on
course for subtle errors
of judgement. At times

she quite lost her sense
of orientation and steered
directly towards disaster,

only contriving to pull
away at the last conceivable
moment. Now Jeanette

pilots her craft more
warily, reminding her-
self to rely neither

on mere habit nor pure
instinct, but at all times
to navigate attentively.

---

despite danger   *joy moving in sincerity*

6. Hail Victory

They staged vast processions
of party-followers to smile, clap,
march, stamp, cheer. Mystical

fervour glistened on uplifted
faces. Young and old, this was
their revolution, never-before-

achieved. And they its whitest
knights, thunder-bearers, light-
bringers, swift-speed-breeders,

joy-symphonisers, harmony-
wreakers, passion-synthesisers,
haulers of heaven here-now,

victory-hailers, cleanser-healers,
erasing all in their way, perfection-
brokers, apocalypse-riders, death-

camp-builders, mass murderers.
May they lie drowning forever in
seething lakes of everlasting fire.

---

these were the 'wing'd-with-awe'   *inviolable*

(59)

Dispersing

wind   *over water*

He watches his friend walk away

He watches his
friend walk away
along the long

straight empty road
and get smaller with
each step, as sun

beats down, smudging
puddles of light onto
blistering tarmac, till

his friend, who was
an upright twig with
twiglet arms, has

become a number
one, a dotted i and
then a set of

blinked flashes
and spots, a blur,
a nothing.

---

wind moves over water   *time to make the long crossing*

1. Scattering

Wind's knife cuts waves,
wounding and dividing some,
scattering others. They rise

like herds, like hordes
of wild white horses, long
manes bobbing, curling.

They gallop, twist, leap, buck
beneath. This ship will ride on
and over, steer through

thick and thin, mount
any storm or tempest that
unthinking Fortune may

throw or thrust upon us.
Now our commander takes
control, by necessity we

too acquire the brute
speed and elegance of strong
beautiful noble horses.

following fortune　　　　　　*with a stallion's strength and patience*

2. Escaping

Through mosquito-infested
marshland we led our horses
not daring mount them, for

they would have sunk beneath
our weight. Wind blew up, rain
spattered then drenched us

to shivering skins. We had
no words of any kind, nothing
to say, but our teeth rattled

and chattered in our mouths
like loose pebbles on a riverbed.
Now our horses will carry us

across sierras blond with dust,
past giant anthills and prickly pears,
to valleys where peaches grow.

Pull down your kerchief
over your eyes. Wind a scarf
around your neck.

---

escaping at the right moment   *without regret*

3. At marriage-end

We aren't much,
you and I, under the sun's
eye, ripples of wind

on water, quick
to disappear. This is
our storm's end and

hope's beginning. Duty
can't keep us together, nor
laws made by others,

nor our own willpower.
We came together in blood
and fire. We've stayed

together through drought
and ice. My hope is our first
lost gentleness now

may rest in each of us
quiet, as now for ever we
go our separate ways.

4. River-run, river-ruin

Always light-crazed,
longing for lowest places,
you who tunnelled under

ground, rose in fountains,
descended in huge trunks
and columns of ever-

moving drapery sculpted
out of time, poured down
huge volumes, and so

grew from first trick-
lings to an empire of water –
how quiet and gentle now

you spread your branches
at your delta, silt sands up
into islands, and disperse

your being with no regret
or sadness, as you bleed out
back timelesss to sea.

---

dispersing then reuniting   *stronger than a fortress*

476

5. For Natalie, dying

As mist on morning's
horizon, and layers
that hover on fields

and droplets combed
minutely from foam
on curling waves

evaporate in wind
and are lifted higher
than mountains

so cloud will return
to sea, as sea
will return to sky

and sunlight dissolve them
and clarify all tumbling
and rising shadows.

Come, then
Natalie, pass
through gently

---

dispersing a queen's belongings   *as time itself dissolves*

6. Rowan tree, the day after her departure

Shimmer of wind
through leaves of this
my doom-tree

laden with
red September berries
outside our window

restores me
back to being, brings
me from believing

all order had collapsed –
to being back in our
more-or-less shared

and recognisable world
even though we're all
visitors and the same

wind will snuffle every
one of us some
time for good out of it.

(60)

Restricting

water   *in the lake*

Economies

Work clean, keen,
straight. Earn your
pay. Yet realise

love admits no
wage claims, overtime
bonuses, perks, rights,

manager's profits,
chairman's investment,
bureaucrat's ploy.

The more you earn
the more you have your
self: Caesar's code.

But love's morse
patters its SOS in
the living heart's

continuous present:
the more you give out
yourself the finer.

1. In a monastery garden

Against these walls
wisteria, honeysuckle, clematis
and varied wandering ivies

curl and twist
spiralling tendrils. Woody gnarls
push up delicate green

feelers. Ages ago, monks
planted these wall-huggers, as
if to remind themselves

how such plants, even
though dependent and spending
much time in shadow

thrive on a cultivation
so quiet and patient their slow
determined thrust may seem

almost a permanence.
Coiling, tenacious, they grip
cement and brickwork

2. Rodney

Rod preferred to stay at
home, pottering around
house and garden. He

could have explored
and had plenty of good
opportunities to do so

but got frightened of
trying anything without
family or friends, who

encouraged him well
enough. More and more
stubborn, quirky, blunt,

he ignored chances, in-
cluding crucial advice, to
show up. Now thickened,

dulled, clogged, he's like
a lukewarm stagnant pool
no fresh streams nourish.

---

over-restricting   *himself*

3. Izzie

Izzie risks overflowing all
edges, frontiers, shorelines,
including those of her

own flesh, heart, blood, as
if she lived in Never-Never-
Land, not in this here-now

acute-and-fresh-wounded
by interlayered no-go zones,
hemmed in by endless

coils of numbers, beings,
things, sealed by prepositions,
dialectics, spacetime, death,

and hounded by Ananke's
pack baying and howling be-
hind her. When this flood

of hers subsides, will she
recognise where her bounds,
her bonds, were, should be?

---

entire absence   *of restriction*

4. Tidying up, clearing out

Now it's good
to clear the house of
everything not

needed, especially
pots, pans, pictures,
baskets, ornaments,

books that won't
be looked at again, gone
hopes, obsolete dreams.

Some things will go to
children or grandchildren,
some to charity.

From now on self
will be surrounded
by a very few

loved and familiar
objects and still fewer
impossible desires.

5. On Mill Road

Apples are ripening
on their trees. Sam walks
up Mill Road to do

his shopping at the
Co-op and post three
letters. Then calls in

at greengrocer's
and buys a small bundle
of fresh parsley. Sees

a neighbour and they
chat a bit. Summer air tastes
delicious. Walking is

good for breathing.
He enjoys it. Eyes keep on
being amazed at things

they see and hear. Heart
for now goes on beating
alert and strong.

6. Stacey

It wasn't a good idea to
go on doing the same thing
year in year out, believing

at first she could/might
'do' better, which later (too
late) mutated into could/

might 'have done'. So
Stacey's grammar of self-
waste got generated from

possibility, through unreal
wish and longing, to impasse,
actual impossibility, plus

alternate self-revelling,
self-revealing, self-reviling,
in hypothetical pasts.

A dried husk of a self
shrivelled in remorse and
regret is all that remains.

(61)

Inner Trusting

wind   *ruffles the lake*

Ring of truth

Wind over lakes
whips still water
in shimmerings

fleshing out
puffed and engorged
bodies of clouds

ripping them
into storms that tear
sky's face open

to fill out rivers,
deepen wells, nourish
desert places

till what was dispersed
is regathered, and what
was lost, recollected.

There is no end.
Through pain and passion
quietness endures.

1. Inanna's descent

She climbed down
past lies and lives. She
held her breath until

she reached where
skin is not and bone is
not and spirit hangs

on an endless
thread twined thousands
of times finer than

a hair's breadth, a
neutron's breath, a quark's
bark, no more than

the yocto-width of a silent
sighless sigh. And somehow
there her self held

onto her spirit and she
returned to flesh, breath,
world, this, making.

2. Seagull's wings

For an instant
beating
seagull's wings

take up the whole
sky. This heaven-
filling happens

both at zenith and nadir
of their pulsing and
drumming on wind.

Time, unstitched
from history, goes
into reverse. At the

ferry's stern we stand,
so wholly held by this
watching, that distances

slip into haze. Everything
broken is mended. Where we
are is the horizon.

---

3. At Shipwreck Head

In this bay
sea always screams
into wind, copying

gulls. It never lets up.
Here many ships went
down. This narrow

channel between land
and submerged ridge of
razor-edged rock

axed hulls of wood
to splinters, hacking and
tearing through steel

like lightning. A place
not conducive to peaceful
thinking, therefore one

of the aptest to brood
over ends and beginnings,
ways within ways.

---

now drums now hushes   *now sobs now sings*

4. In peaceful night

In peaceful
night no-one
disturbs but

unplaceable voices
calling words
from an unknown

language in his
own head
which he knows

he understands and
speaks, even though never
how. Light a candle,

they call. On
this your table
in this your air

over this your
sorrow before
this your grave

---

moon   *nearly full*

5. Ghost, revisiting

Greetings, ghost, father.
So you have come back –
immaculately groomed

in double-breasted suit,
ironed shirt, lapis lazuli
cufflinks, discreetly

knotted navy tie,
brown and white spats.
This time you've no

instrument to play. I
say, *Your cello's still here,*
waiting. But you prefer

to ask questions of me.
We sit facing each other
at the kitchen table in

our old house in
Wentworth Road.
Joy. Amazement.

6. Ghost, questioning

Blandly you smile. So *you*
are a poet, you say. *So tell me,*
are you a good poet? A test.

I look you in the eyes.
If I'm good isn't for me to say.
But I'm a true poet. You

smile, eyebrows raised. It's
time to go. *Don't tell your mother,*
you say. *It's you I came for.*

Through the old scullery, past
the serving-hatch to our dining
room, with its dark brown

leather-seated chairs, I walk
behind you down the long hall.
Polite, mute, I see you out

as if you were a stranger
Closing the front door, I stand
behind it, weeping.

(62)

Overstepping

thunder   *over the mountain*

What our messenger bird said

What instructions or
news did our messenger
bird bring us, friend?

A minuscule scrolled
message strapped to its leg
packed with words: Keep

head down, out of sight.
Don't go forward, onward,
or higher. This is not

time for large ambitious
leaps. Take exercise, bring
top-heavy weight

of upper body
down to strengthen feet,
calves, thighs. Practise

small precise figures.
Have all your utensils
clean, polished, ready.

1. Bird up there black

That bird up there
black black black
because of the sun

behind it, is
flying straight
on arcs of air

into death. Suddenly
there will be total
airlessness in its

tiny sturdy lungs and
all its flights forever
stop. As if the sun

had swallowed it,
it will be devoured
in fire. It will dissolve

in your blinded eyes
when you dare look
straight at the sun.

bird flying, far   *too high*

497

2. Timbre of her voice

And now he meets his
dead mother, for whom in
life he had scant respect.

She is neither young
nor old, but both and each
at once. She belongs

neither to this time
nor any other. She is himself
and in himself, yet separate.

And mother now assumes
simple control and directs
attention to getting

small things done right.
This way, she says. *Look!*
And this! Curious after

so many years since her
death, to hear the timbre
of her voice so clearly.

meeting not father   *but mother*

3. Looking for [the] Revolution

Brave Iulian Shchutskii,
sinologist, historian, translator,
knew Manchu, Mandarin,

Cantonese, Mongolian, Viet-
namese, Japanese, German and
English. Researched the *I Ching*.

His favourite joke: a Russian,
up a pole, scans [the] horizon
for [the] Revolution. When

asked to come down, the
Russian refuses, this being his
'permanent full-time job'.

For this, for being who
and what he was, Shchutskii
incurred Stalin's wrath, got

arrested by NKVD (1937)
and perished (1938) aged 41,
skull crushed by a chain.

---

struck down   *from above and behind*

4. She does her job

The people she
works for exploit
and despise her.

They see of her
what they need,
her usable skills.

To them harmony
between humans and
nature is irrelevant.

So she doesn't use
more words than needed,
avoids gossip, keeps

thoughts to herself,
does her job and does
it pretty but not

very or exceedingly
well. Waits. Gets paid.
Grits her teeth.

5. A marksman

Great stuff. No, no birds
to shoot at up there in the sky
today. Cloud's too thick,

though there's no rain.
But look, here's one sitting
in a cave like a ruddy great

bat. Tempting fate. Fetch
torches then, yeomen, torch-
men, henchmen, so His

Royal Highness can get in
a good popshot and bag at least
one today. Ho Ho well well

Bingo Stingo. See it flut-
ter down dead. I say jolly
well done Petit Prince.

It was a huge white
owl. What kind of an
achievement is that?

---

our prince shoots a bird   *in a cave*

6. Bird falling out of sky

So too when I fly
or fall into my own
death all thoughts

ideas words music
will flutter or drop
to the ground plop

plummeting into
completion smashing
into perfection. Just like

that bird, into the blasting
ring of the sun. Stench
of frazzled feathers

and shit and blood will get
cleaned. Though that burning
is not hard to see, my mind

completely fails to conceive
of its own non-being
before birth returning.

flying bird   *runs out of sky*

502

(63)

After Crossing Over

---

water

over fire

Odyssified

Thrown off balance by being
snug, smug, homebound, he has
to go abroad again. No choice.

Last journey done, what
next? Same voice calling – new
sunsets, archipelagos, islands,

continents, rainbows? In Ithaca,
bed-ridden, his condition worsens.
But wordless heartsong buzzes,

awakening him. Before dawn he
tiptoes through palace gates unseen
humming down to harbour.

Now he's caulked leaks,
greased rowlocks, uncoiled ropes,
weighed anchor, loosened sails –

off again, zones unknown,
ocean in head, ways in spirit,
ban regret, bar returning.

1. Fording

There being no bridge
or ferry, crossing meant
fording, a wary carrying

of weapons and wares
with hands held above heads,
planting each footstep in

moving mud, taking
weight on flexible knees,
steadfast breath deeper,

before sluggishly scuff-
ing other leg forward, as if
emptied, every muscle

blazing through swirl
of juddering currents, then
finally into shallows, to

slice through water as
if burdened bodies were
paper blades, gold leaf.

little fox, careful   *still has to wet his tail*

2. In faint distress

Hwat hath Madam lost?
Hir jewels? Hatte? Veyle? Or
Could it perchance be

hir wigg? Bing bong
have we (or not) entered
slapstick? A moralised

Punch & Judy? Or a
test of hir *virtu*? And who
might culprit be other

than hir *housbounde*?
Bring on policing amper-
sands! Supported by

asterisks! She will not
be *permitted* to follow
path(s) of evil. All will

come to hir ayde, they
that robbed hir will fle
and naane dar retorne.

she'll get it all back   *in less than a week*

3. Merlin to young Arthur

If and when success
seems graspable, maintain
calm. Keep constant

watch for tricksters
who come across as
friends. What you

can achieve will elude
you far longer than you
expected. Obstacles

and enemies will rot
roofbeams and rafters,
tumble tiles on your

head. Let patience be
order of your days in all
seasons. Anticipate

moves of enemies,
low and inflated. Never
use force lightly.

to conquer and pacify   *a kingdom takes years*

4. Necessary repairs

Our junk lies on her side,
battered by her last crossing.
Not surprising, considering

what rose up against her –
unpredicted winds, waves
like whirling mountains,

currents dizzying, crazed,
as out of nightmare. Time
for patient mending –

hull, keel, tiller, masts,
welding, sealing, painting –
for she will carry us over

many more seas. With
each creak and shudder of
her aged joints, we shall

ache and smart with her,
as old pains shoot through
her long-memoried scars.

caulking leaks   *refurbishing*

5. In negative

Stars puckered on night,
extreme white on extreme black,
first settling snowflakes,

powder of white shadow
sprinkled on black light, all
these I saw. Then,

in an eyeblink, in
negative, a sapphire sun
in a black sky. And

hairs on my dead arms
stood, I no astronomer, nor
filigree mesh-twister.

Time slowed, was no
more. Now how can there be
no now-any-more? I go

into the dustless zone
into gone deathcall, calling
Glad to have lived.

---

burning herbs, a ceremony   *simple in thanks and praise*

6. First bricks

When I realised I'd
hardly started working
out or on foundations

this declared itself
complete. It did so
with no fanfare or

furore, astonishingly
quiet. Time to move on
then. To shaping and

choosing first bricks
for ground floor. Now
may this go on and

out even to shadow-
land, and know the fire
ever inside no matter

how much death or
many deaths need be
absorbed on its way.

wetting one's head   *one job done, now for the next*

(64)

Before crossing over

---

fire   *over water*

Fire-tail

Fox, little fire-tail, not
really ready to cross such a
broad flooded river, not

yet big or strong enough
for this biggest test of all,
now you've trodden a

fine fierce line between
moving forward bravely,
sensibly, carefully, and

taking a fat reckless
plunge, gambling, getting
in over your head. Never

mind, there'll be more
chances later, to try again
when you're a bit more

savvy, stronger, and
waters aren't so full. No
harm done. Not yet.

1. Fox (again) on river-bank

Little fire-tailed fox, now
you've really gone and done it,
taken your big brave plunge,

got ducked under water
way over your head. Soaked
right through, sozzled, you

almost could have drowned.
So do you need us to clap you?
Cheer you? Console you?

Weep and wail? Or what?
Now you've turned to face us,
big ears pricked forward,

how stupid and sheepish
you look, shivering on your
bank. Time, brave little fox,

to work out currents and
rivers, think through seasons
and tides, get wise to things.

this time   *got wet through*

2. In rat-light

In rat-light a torch pierces
angles not glimpsed in centuries.
But such peering can

hardly count as seeing.
Tiger's eyes see through dark.
Dragon's eyes cast mirrors

into mirrors' mirrors. Words
melt through, though you thought
them your all. When bubbles

burst, what they held falls away
for good. But what words entailed,
entangled in dank air, hangs

around ages. Don't inhale it.
Let it fall viral in ghost-caves.
Let it dissolve in water.

Clarified mind returns
breath to source. Pouring breath
back there turns light around.

---

3. Eyes open forward

Some hesitate, some
look back. Which isn't the
right thing now. Always

they will need to go
back. *Again, again,* they'll
call and be called.

Some wait, eyes closed,
appealing or quiescent,
downcast or uplifted,

hopeless or sure, and
so passive. I'd wish to be
among those who keep

eyes open forward,
peripheries sharpened, not
hoping but emptied,

alert for whatever, for
the next, and afternext,
for the unexpected.

4. Ready steady go

More and more stitches
in this tapestry? Language
like life is *infectious*. Bees

swarm in these eaves
and summer caves in on
itself. What seemed

to constitute silence
seams overbrimming
words until no more

are needed. Until no
way more is, or are. Here we
are again, like children

about to cross The Road,
looking both ways, ready.
Say, old friend, I don't

know where we're
going. That's more or less
all I do know. *Hah!*

5. Alchymical Perle

Axiomatic, our *precious*
perle wythouten spotte is to be
found at home, in our own

hearth, heart, guts. And in
core of commonplace, among
ordinary (ornery) things

is where we're to look
again and again, before our
noses, behind our backs,

in and through darkest
deepest blind spots. What
at first seemed simple

may turn out quite
complex – yet simplicity
and complexity keep

opening out into each
other, interpenetrating,
blurring, irradiating.

6. Brightness diffusing

Sunlight bronzes sea.
Everything sighs. Mid-
October, still warm.

Olive leaves' undersides,
dull metallic sheens, flicker
across sandy hill groves.

Our sunflower heads
are harvested. Light flames
oleanders and cypresses.

Prickly pears swell,
lobes topping green oval
faces, golden grenades.

Instress, pattern, glory.
It all coheres, no question,
as do these notes of mine.

Come sit at the table
out here on the balcony.
Drink a glass of wine.

Postscript

Changing is conceived as a single work, a composite poem made up of many small poems. It is based closely on the Chinese *Book of Changes* or the *I Ching*, and it is intended in part as an act of homage to this ancient text.[1] But while many of its parts are rooted in the *I Ching*, and most take their inspiration from it and make repeated reference to it, and while its overall concept, plan, structure and themes have been configured through the *I Ching*, *Changing* is not a translation or a commentary. My hope is that this book will be read first and foremost as a poem, or gathering of poems, in its own right and for its own sake.

The *I Ching* is one of the most extraordinary books of all time. It possesses a history unlike any other work of comparable stature in any language or culture. Its earliest known version, the *Zhouyi*, which belongs to the Chinese Bronze Age, is nearly three thousand years old. The text was originally conceived, composed and compiled as a divination manual, that is, as a handbook for fortune-telling. It reflects earlier magical and religious practices whose deepest roots lie so far back in time that it is impossible to say when they originated: they certainly go back to the Neolithic age. Fortune-telling is a function that the *I Ching* still serves today.[2]

One of the other most interesting and powerful aspects of even the earliest version of the *I Ching* is its perfectly symmetrical patterning. It is structured into sixty-four interconnecting and interdependent chapters, units or clusters. Each of these contains six components: hence the adoption of

---

[1] The ancient Chinese text 易經 is known in English by various titles, such as *The Changes*, *Change*, the *Classic of Change*, and the *I Ching* (sometimes abbreviated to the *I*) or *Yijing* (the *Yi*). These last are transliterations of the Chinese name, the former in the older Wade-Giles system and the latter in the pinyin system which was officially adopted in China in 1982. Following long-established English practice, here I use the term *I Ching*. For other transliterations from Chinese, I use pinyin. For the earliest known version of the *I Ching*, I use the accepted name, the *Zhouyi*.

[2] See Richard J. Smith, 1991, *Fortune-Tellers and Philosophers: Divination in Traditional Chinese Society* (Taipei: SMC Publishing).

the English term 'hexagram', a unit or set which can in turn be divided into two constitutive parts called 'trigrams'. In divination, an individual reading is obtained by chance permutations of a relatively simple set of instructions, which usually involves manipulating a set of sticks or tossing three coins. The *I Ching*'s overall mathematical structure, which is based on the simplest of binary principles, generates a large number of combinations. Once one of these has been selected, and once it has been activated by being intermeshed, as it were, with a diviner's specific question, it is capable of producing a set of interpretations that is (or appears to be) both specific and relevant to that question. Since each question put to it is itself unique, while the *I Ching* never loses its formal elegance or integrity, its capacity to generate unique interpretations and applications is endless.

Thanks in large part to this mathematically-based generative power, the *Zhouyi* quickly attracted extensive explications and philosophical commentaries. Between around 800 BCE and around 300 BCE, some of these were appended to the original text, to make up the *I Ching* as we know it today. By 136 BCE, the entire body of material that by then constituted this corpus was established in Imperial China as the first and foremost among the Confucian 'classics'. This elevation to the highest status possible in the Imperial canon signified that the *I Ching* required devotion, attention, questioning, clarification and reinterpretation. Over succeeding centuries, commentary and exegesis proliferated; and reference to the *I Ching* as an eminently quotable source of wisdom and common sense became standard cultural procedure in China. Meanwhile, knowledge and use of the text gradually spread to other countries, including, Korea, Japan and Vietnam.

In the last years of the seventeenth century, Jesuit missionaries brought copies of the *I Ching* to France and translations began to appear in European languages, including Latin. Around the mid-twentieth century, the *I Ching*'s aleatory aspects began to interest writers, composers and artists in Western society; and in the nineteen-sixties, thanks to its spiritual and mysterious qualities, the text quickly connected, as if by magnetic attraction, with the aspirations and longings of many young people.

In the nineteen-seventies, the Chinese soil yielded up a spate of stupendous archaeological discoveries, the most dramatic of which occurred in 1974 when the 'Terracotta Army', a vast array of buried sculptures, was unearthed in the tomb of the Emperor Qin Shi Huang (260–210 BC) at Lintong. From the point of view of ancient divinatory texts, within the two decades between the nineteen-seventies and nineteen-nineties, at least four other scarcely less exciting excavations have revolutionised scholarship. These have included partial or complete versions of the *Zhouyi* and other ancient texts concerned with divination. The first and most famous of these, a manuscript of the *Zhouyi* written on silk, was discovered in 1974 at Mawangdui ['King Ma's Mound'].[3] Together, these discoveries have thrown new light on the *I Ching* and on ancient divination practices, provoking even more new questions than they have revealed answers.

For more than two millennia, no book in human history other than the Bible has attracted more commentaries, interpretations, debates, controversies, editions and translations. Today the *I Ching* remains as puzzling, challenging, thought-provoking and exciting as ever, and thanks to these major recent archaeological finds, its study is an open field that continues to widen and deepen.[4]

I first came across the *I Ching* in 1962, when I was a nineteen-year-old undergraduate studying English at Cambridge: that is, just over fifty-four years ago at the time of writing this. It has fascinated me ever since and has constantly pulled me back into it. Like many others in my generation, I began to consult the book for divination and intermittently kept up the practice for many years. More recently, I have spent a good deal of time exploring various versions of the text and aspects of its history, consulting translations, analyses and commentaries. The final shape and content of *Changing* have emerged out of both aspects of this involvement.

The *I Ching* operates transversally to sequential linearity. It cuts across both logical and narrative modes, intersecting them by applying a mode of thinking and perception – and hence also, by invoking a way of being – that is irreducibly synthetic, correlative, resonant, and poetic. To amplify these remarks: the *I Ching* does not function primarily in the way that any myth, tale, story or novel must proceed and operate, even though it may admit all such narrative elements. Nor is it 'rooted' in one or more particular places, as all fictions necessarily are. Nor does it proceed in the manner of a developing

---

[3] For English translations of these texts, with extended discussions, analyses and commentaries, see the pioneering work of Edward L. Shaughnessy, especially in his *I Ching, the Classic of Change: the first English translation of the newly discovered second-century B. C. Mawangdui texts*, 1996 (New York, NY: Ballantine Books) and *Unearthing the Changes*, 2013 (New York: Columbia University Press).

[4] For a concise history of the book, see Richard J. Smith, *The I Chjing, a Biography*, 2012 (Princeton, NJ: Princeton University Press).

argument. Consisting primarily of visual symbols patterned on binary mathematical options, which are combined with verbal 'images', 'statements' and 'judgements', it is, rather, a generative and transformative structure which remains entirely passive and latent until it is 'activated'. But once this happens, it presents itself as immediately available for *practical application in the field of now*, in and through which it creates a flow of information for and through its user. As I have suggested, this information flow is based on a set of pre-formulated binary conversion rules which at their basic level are extremely simple. In this respect, the *I Ching* functions like (as) a kind of proto-computer. What 'switches on' the *I Ching* is the personal user's asking of a question in the first phase of the divination procedure. Use of the word *user* here reiterates the prime intended function of the *I Ching*, in contradistinction to any other books of comparable intellectual and imaginative scope, reach or magnitude in world history. It is a manual.

The *I Ching* is notoriously 'difficult' for all kinds of reasons. One is that the text itself is not stable. It exists in many versions, and there is no single 'original'. Another is that over more than two millennia, the Chinese language has changed in countless ways. A further point is that the differences between ancient Chinese and modern English are enormous and no translation can capture *all* the associations of ancient Chinese words and graphs. What is more, polysemy, ambiguity and the syncretic layering of potential meanings are all built into the *I Ching* as necessary elements, simply because any mantic fortune-telling text needs to be applicable to as wide a variety of situations and interpretable in as many ways as possible. If and where the *I Ching* lacks literal surface clarity, it compensates by echoic resonance.

The first poem I wrote directly 'out of' the *I Ching* was 'Two lakes, joined', on August 30, 1984 (see p. 464). The piece, which was based on a divination, articulated itself quickly and effortlessly through composition into its particular form, with little need for restructuring or rewriting. This led to more poems, all patterned on the structure that had emerged during composition of this first one. Gradually, these pieces accumulated in notebooks. By the 1990s, I was beginning to entertain the idea of writing a collection based on the *I Ching*, and in 2002 I made a first attempt at gathering some of these pieces together. They appeared under the title 'Following' in *Book With*

No Back Cover (David Paul, London, 2003). So the formative background to *Changing* extended over fifty years. The actual writing occurred between the mid-1980s and 2014, and I was most actively absorbed in its composition between 2010 and 2014.

I have modelled *Changing* closely on the *I Ching* by replicating and adapting its architectonic patterns at various levels of compositional structure. At the micro-level, based on the simple form that emerged spontaneously through the composition of 'Two lakes, joined', each poem has six stanzas and each stanza consists of three lines. In this way, the forms of both hexagram and trigram are implicitly re-presented (re-called, re-embodied, reduplicated, replicated, etc.) in each poem's *mise-en-page*. The visual and formal pattern-ing of six tercets (eighteen lines) also suggests three hexagrams stacked over one another.

At the macro-level, the book consists of sixty-four clusters of poems, each re-presenting a hexagram. Each cluster begins with an italicised 'head-poem', which is related thematically to its corresponding hexagam title and statement in the *I Ching*, and each of these is followed by six further numbered poems corresponding structurally (and often, though not always, thematically too) to the hexagram's six change-lines. In this way, each of the *I Ching*'s hexagrams yields a cluster of seven poems, arranged hierarchically and in a sequence that follows that of the 'received' (standard) version. Together with two additional poems for the *I Ching*'s extra line-readings in the first two hexagrams, the number of poems in the book is (64 x 7) + 2 = 450.

In modelling the sixty-four cluster titles, as well as the title *Changing* itself, I have consistently deployed English words ending in '-*ing*' in order to reflect (refract, inflect), even if only in part, the complex polysemies of Chinese graphs that serve as hexagram names in the *I Ching*. Each poem also has a 'base-line', which is both an integral part of its text and serves as a gloss on it. Most (though not all) base-lines connect the poem directly with the *I Ching*.

I have found the *I Ching* itself compelling both as a source and as a ground for poetry, and especially for a long poem. Its symmetrical structure itself suggests not only an over-arching 'pattern' or 'frame' but one that has no need to be dependent on the Aristotelian unities of time and place or, for that matter, on any other kind of insistent narrative or dramatic form. What is more, given a patterning principle like that of the *I Ching*, the kinds of modes, models and devices that have developed out of the great Symbolists, Modernists and Surrealists as 'connecting' principles – such as associative linkage, parataxis, focus on the 'arbitrariness' of language, or attentive highlighting of the apparent gulf between the *signifiant* and *signifié*, and so on – may all be included in the scope of the work, but need neither to be exclusively relied on nor to be slavishly copied. As for associative, analogical or correlative thinking, sometimes also known as 'correlative cosmos-building', this is not only the mental foundation for poetry, ritual and magic in all societies, but specifically underpins the holistic vision of the universe that runs through all traditional Chinese thought – most evidently so in Daoism. It also gives rise to C. G. Jung's theory of synchronicity, which is itself rooted in the *I Ching*. Above all, the *I Ching*'s ambiguities and necessary openness to polysemic inter-pretation are inherently poetic. Just as in dream interpretation, even when an initial surface reading of the *I Ching* seems evident or 'clearly' applicable, syncretic layering and variation are always readily available to modify, expand and deepen it, in ways that may be either subtle or dramatic, and are usually unexpected.

Mention of dream reopens a fuller dimension. The *I Ching*'s original mantic purpose was to unlock the mysterious secrets of time, to peer into the future, and to interpret the apparently unfathomable patterns of destiny.

⸻

If any single motif or symbol in the *I Ching* has most come to represent the *I Ching* in my own mind, it is that of the well (hexagram 48). The Chinese graph 井 (*jing*) is an idealised pictorial representation of a well in the centre of eight fields or farms. It originates in the ancient feudal practice called the 'well-field' system: 井田 (*jing tian*). Fields or farms were divided into nine equally sized square areas, with eight families tilling one outer area each, while the ninth, the central one that belonged to the feudal overlord, was cultivated by all eight families.[5] In some early representations, a small black dot is present at the centre of the graph to represent the well itself. In *Changing*, the title I have chosen for 井 (*Jing*) is 'Welling, Replenishing', and the group of poems devoted to this hexagram is intended to explore the motif both at its literal surface and at various levels of its symbolic resonance, including the dominant one of the *I Ching* itself as source and resource. This procedure, I hope, may also both engender and typify a reading of *Changing*

---

[5] See Fung Yu-Lan, 1983, *A History of Chinese Philosophy*, tr. Derk Bode, vol. 1 (Princeton, NJ: Princeton University Press): pp. 10-13.

as a self-commenting, self-reflecting, reverberating, echoic system. In the same way that looking down into a well filled with water under sunlight facilitates visual reflection – not to mention mental reflection (on heights, depths, and their relative perspectives) – and just as calling down into a well sets up echoic resonance, so my hope is that *Changing* may both *reflect and echo itself* to a reader while it is being read, and so enable the reader to reflect *on* it, just as I also hope it may reflect and echo (*and* enable the reader to reflect on) the material it integrates, the processes of its own making, and its own 'deep' source, the *I Ching*.

When I began writing poems related to the *I Ching*, I knew next to nothing about the ancient text. Now that *Changing* has been completed – or rather, has completed itself – I have the increasing sense of the *Book of Changes* opening out on even richer, deeper, more extraordinary and dazzlingly exciting fields than it could possibly have hinted at in 1962 when I first met the text, at the age of nineteen. Yet I also think now that if, when I started writing *Changing*, I had known what I know now about the *I Ching* – which is still not very much – the poem I would have set out to write would have been very different. Might it have been a 'better' poem? Perhaps it might. But perhaps, lacking the charge of discovery that ignorance donates so freely and with such overwhelmingly fierce generosity to any absolute beginner, particularly when young, I might not even have started to write it at all. So here, then, the book's close, which is a non-finishing and an un-ending, delivers its unpredicted and unforeseen openings. The future is always the strongest of all attractors and beginnings are precisely where, again and again, the *I Ching* always locates itself.[6]

RB
CAMBRIDGE
JULY 15, 2014

---

[6] I intend to provide a more detailed account of connections between *Changing* and the *I Ching* in a separate book of essays. This will explore aspects of composition procedures by outlining ways in which *Changing* is modelled on the *I Ching* and mapped back onto it, both structurally and thematically. It will also contain essays on the history of the *I Ching*, the issue of 'difficulty' in and associated with the text, and explorations of some of the ways in which the *I Ching* relates to poetic thinking.

Acknowledgements

My thanks to the editors who have previously published the following poems: 'Decay', 'The nonplussed pleasures of love', 'Lean and strong', 'Untouchable light, miraculous air' (under the title 'Untouchable, miraculous air')', 'Bird up there black', and 'He left his city', with Chinese translations by Chee Lay Tan, *Poetry Sky*, 2005, online at http://www.poetrysky. com/quarterly/quarterly-richardburns.html; 'Dawn' in *Light Unlocked*, Enitharmon Press, London, 2005; 'TRAVELLING' (1-6), *Wasafiri* 57, Spring 2009; 'She sweeps shadows', 'At least one of the liars', 'Consultation of the diagrams', 'Small poem for Gully' (under the title 'Poem for Gully'), 'A good general' (under the title 'A good general 1'), and 'A modest man' (under the title 'A good general 2'), *Shearsman* 83 & 84, Summer, 2010; 'Order in grand design', 'Everyone knows the ways', 'When she sang in the bazaar', 'When she sang in the white alley', and 'After the Massacre', *Notre Dame Review* 30, Summer/Fall 2010; 'Meditation at Hourn Farm' and 'Nothing happens', *Dragon's Mouth*, 2011: 1; 'Language palazzo', 'The prime-minister heliports', 'Heroes, heroines', 'Mist dispersing', 'Like dew upon the morning', and 'In the spirit of Walt Whitman', *Spokes Poetry*, August 2013, online at http://www.simegen.com/writers/spokes/Spokes%202012/spokes_ page_03.html; 'BITING THROUGH', *Notre Dame Review* 37, Winter 2013; 'Thirty-six Just Men', *Jewish Quarterly* 61[1], Spring 2014; 'Thesaurus', 'Morning, open windows', 'Winter Solstice', '*C'est la vie, mort de la Mort*', 'Beautiful September Morning', and 'Brightness Diffusing', *The Fortnightly Review*, June 2014, online at http://fortnightlyreview.co.uk/2014/06/ richard-berengarten/; 'Child survivor's testimony', *European Judaism* 47: 14[2]; 'She wrote herself into Death', *Oxford Magazine* 350, 2014; 'Light fills and fails' and 'The force that fills and empties', *Agenda* 48 [1-2], 2014; 'Getting Down In', 'She Sweeps Shadows', 'When Hope Ended', and 'Old Washerwoman', *Urthona* 31, 2014; 'WELLING, REPLENISHING', *Golden Handcuffs Review* 20, Spring 2015; 'BEGINNING' and 'BRINGING UP', *Contrapasso* 8, Spring 2015; 'DARKENING', *Molly Bloom* 7, May 2015; 'FALLING', *Molly Bloom* 8, September 2015; 'Child Survivor's Testimony' in *Liberation*, Beacon Press, Boston, 2015; 'Indelible shadows tattooed', 'Untouchable light, miraculous air', and 'No Horizon at Trabzen', *Earl of Seacliff Art Workshop Broadsheet 17*, 2016; and 'Light fills and fails', *Jewish Quarterly* 63[3], Autumn 2016.

Some of the poems in this volume had a trial run in the sequence 'Following' in *Book With No Back Cover*, David Paul, London, 2003. Several poems appear in other previous collections: 'Two lakes, joined', under the title 'Two lakes', in *For the Living*, 2011; 'Decay,' under the title 'Stagnation', as the opening poem in *The Blue Butterfly*, and 'Under hills', under the title 'Grace', as the concluding poem in the same volume, 2011, pp. 3 and 106 respectively; and 'Seagull's wings' and 'Apple', under the title 'The Apple', in *Under Balkan Light*, 2011, pp. 30 and 133 respectively. 'The minister has been tainted' appears, in different format, in *The Manager*, 2011, p. 115; as does 'In the primary school' in *Manual*, 2014, p. 55. All these books are published by Shearsman Books.

I should also like to express my warmest thanks to the many friends, colleagues and teachers who have helped, encouraged and advised me during the long process of writing this book. In particular, for first introducing me to the *I Ching* in 1963 when we were undergraduates together at Cambridge, my life-long gratitude goes to John Blackwood (1943–1993). I should also like to thank my former wife, Kim Landers, with whom I shared that introduction and took first steps in exploring the *I Ching* in the Wilhelm-Baynes translation.

For cultivation in several Chinese arts and disciplines, I am deeply grateful to Alastair Reid for teaching me the *taijiquan* form which he learned from his teacher Rose Li (Li Shaoqiang, c. 1914–2001); to Wang Zhixing for his introduction to *huagong,* his version of *qigong;* to Shi Jing, Shi Dao, and friends and colleagues at the British Taoist Association for preliminary guidance and instruction in Daoist meditation and *dao yin*; to Robert Peng for his *qi*-based encouragement; and to Shen Jin for introducing me to the first elements of the comprehensive *qigong* and *taijiquan* system originated by her father, Dr. Shen Hongxun (1939–2011). For a wealth of insights and discoveries over many years derived from being a regular recipient of acupuncture, I should also like to thank Lee Moden, Alan Hext, Françoise Hawkridge and Dr. Wu Jidong.

For an understanding of some linguistic researches into the *I Ching* that have taken place since the 1980s, I was immensely lucky, in 2004, to meet Dr. Richard Kunst and, later, in 2010, Dr. Edward L. Shaughnessy, Professor in Early Chinese Studies at Chicago University. The linguistic archaeology performed in the early 1980s by these pioneering scholars in their Ph.D. theses revolutionised international *I Ching* studies in English by means of close linguistic examinations of its foundation text, the *Zhou Yi*. The work of Kunst and Shaughnessy turned my own thinking about the *I Ching* upside down, and forced me to reappraise and revise all my previous conceptions. See: Edward Louis Shaughnessy, *The Composition of the "Zhouyi"*,

Stanford University; 1983; and Richard Allen Kunst, *The Original "Yijing": A Text, Phonetic Transcription, Translation, and Indexes, with Sample Glosses*, University of California, Berkeley, 1985 (both available from University Microfilms International, Ann Arbor, MI). For Richard Kunst's handwritten notes on the hexagrams, made during his research at Berkeley between 1979 and 1985, see online at http://www.humancomp.org/ftp/yijing/yi_hex.htm. I have also benefited greatly from later email correspondences with Professor Shaughnessy, Dr. Richard J. Smith, Professor of Humanities and Professor of History at Rice University, Texas, and Dr. Bent Nielsen, Associate Professor of Chinese Civilization and Culture at the University of Copenhagen. These three distinguished scholars have been kind enough to read my drafts for essays arising out of the composition of *Changing*, and have given me valuable comments in terms of Sinological scholarship. Above all, it is a huge honour and source of pleasure to me that Professor Shaughnessy has contributed a preface to this book (pp. ix-xix above).

For further occasional advice on aspects of Chinese language, thought, literature and culture, my warm thanks go to Dr. Sally Church, Professor Michael Loewe, Professor David McCullen, and Professor Roel Sterckx, of the Department of East Asian Studies at Cambridge University, and to Dr. John Moffett, librarian at the Joseph Needham Research Institute, Cambridge. I am especially indebted to Dr. Yang Guohua of Downing College, Cambridge, who taught me the basic rules of writing in Chinese, patiently explained to me some of the etymologies and polysemic complexities of the Chinese names for the sixty-four hexagrams, and answered many other linguistic questions. In addition, Dr. Yang helped me settle the title of this book.

My thanks also go to three commentators and translators who have influenced me in their turn in shaping the final version of this book: first, to Dr. Chee Lay Tan, who translated the first selection of some of these poems into Chinese (see above: *Poetry Sky*, 2005) and wrote the first critical essay on the selection published in *Book With No Back Cover* ('Cross-cultural Numerology and Translingual Poetics: Chinese Influences on the Poetry of Richard Berengarten', in *The Salt Companion to Richard Berengarten*, eds. Norman Jope, Paul Scott Derrick and Catherine E. Byfield (Salt Publishing, Cambridge, 2011: 268-286); second, to Wang Bang, who translated twenty of these poems for a bilingual pocket book published by Pulsasir (改 变 / *Changing*, ed. Feng Dong, Hangzhou, 2016); and third, to Dr. Chen Shangzhen, Fellow of the English Poetry Studies Institute (EPSI) at Sun Yat-sen University, Guangzhou, for agreeing to lead a team of translators to translate the entire work into Chinese, and for his textual advice.

For occasional financial support over the years, I am grateful to Astrid Frank, Sir David Garrard, Catherine Ng (Lin Xueqing), and the Royal Literary Fund. Catherine Ng also kindly edited and sponsored a brochure about the book in June 2016 (Los Poetry Press, Cambridge). I should also like to thank the many friends and colleagues who have offered helpful comments and criticism of the texts at various points of composition, especially Anthony Davies, Paul Scott Derrick, Michael Heller, philip kuhn, Kim Landers, Daša Marić, John Matthias, Paschalis Nikolaou, Paul Pines, Michael Rowan-Robinson, Anthony Rudolf, and Carl Schmidt. For researching the German version of the epigraph from C. G. Jung, my particular thanks to Suzanne Bergne.

For this book's visual elements, I am immensely grateful to the poet and calligrapher Dr. Yu Mingquan, Professor at Shandong University of Art and Design, for his renderings of the Chinese title and the hexagram names; to Will Hill for his overall cover design; and to Tony Frazer, the most patient and supportive of publishers and book designers.

Finally, I thank my wife Melanie Rein. As this book's first reader, she has helped me correct and improve many drafts, and has given me her constant support, advice, encouragement and devotion.

RB

CAMBRIDGE

JANUARY 13 2016

Some Translations of the *I Ching*

Among the profusion of translations of the *I Ching* and *Zhouyi* available in English, the following are those that I have most actively and regularly consulted in writing *Changing*.

Blofeld, John. 1991 [1965]. *I Ching, The Book of Change: a New Translation of the Ancient Chinese Text with Detailed Instructions for its Practical Use in Divination* (New York, NY: Penguin Compass).

Feng, Gia-Fu and Jerome Kirk. 1970. *Tai Chi – A Way of Centering & I Ching* (New York, NY: Macmillan).

Huang, Alfred. 2004. *The Complete I Ching* (Rochester, VT: Inner Traditions).

Kunst, Richard Allen. 1985. *The Original "Yijing": A Text, Phonetic Transcription, Translation, and Indexes, with Sample Glosses.* [Ph.D. thesis, University of California at Berkeley, CA] (Ann Arbor, MI: University Microfilms International).

Legge, James. 2007 [1882]. *The I Ching* (Radford, VA: A & D Publishing); first published as *The I Ching, Sacred Books of the East*, Vol. 16, 1889. (Oxford: Oxford University Press). Online at http://www.sacred-texts.com/ich/icap3-2.htm. Reconsulted, August 28, 2015.

Lynn, Richard John. 1994. *The Classic of Changes: a new translation of the I Ching as interpreted by Wang Bi* (New York, NY, & Chichester: Columbia University Press).

Rutt, Richard. 2002 [1996]. *The Book Of Changes (Zhouyi): a Bronze Age Document* (Richmond, VA: Curzon).

Shaughnessy, Edward L. 1996. *I Ching, The Classic of Changes: the First English Translation of the Second Century B.C. Mawangdui Texts* (New York, NY: Ballantine Books).

Wilhelm, Richard. 1970 [1951]. *The I Ching or Book of Changes*, tr. into German, and rendered into English by Cary F. Baynes; foreword by C. G. Jung (London: Routledge & Kegan Paul).

Notes and Dedications

These notes, which include sources and references, are not essential for a reading of the poems, but they may add further dimensions and resonances. The poems originate not only in reading, brooding and mulling over the *I Ching* and other texts, but also in divination and dream, in watching and listening innerly and outerly, and in relationships, friendships and dialogues. Often there is no distinction between these groupings: they overlap, mix, mesh, interpenetrate, bond, bind. And since so many of these poems have arisen out of reciprocity, conviviality, and shared interests and influences, they have often been flighted with personal dedications. In order to avoid interference for a reader, these dedications are presented below, with page references, rather than on the same pages as the texts themselves.

FRONT COVER
The meanings of the Chinese word *yi* 易 include 'change, exchange, barter' as well as 'easy, amiable, lenient'. For discussion on its etymology, see the note on pp. 563-4 to the last poem in this book, p. 518. The calligraphy here, as throughout the book is by Yu Mingquan.

p. 1, EPIGRAPHS
(1) The opening line of the *Dao De Jing*, attributed to Laozi. I have construed this as: "The way that can be wayed is not the Way of Ways." The homophone 'weighed' may also be apt. This interpretation is based on A. C. Graham's brilliant *aperçu*: "The Way that can be 'Way'-ed [formulated in words as the Way] is not the constant Way." See his *Disputers of the Tao*, 2003 (Peru, IL: Open Court Publishing): p. 287.
(2) "By changing it rests." Heraclitus, *On the Universe*, LXXXIII, tr. W. H. S. Jones. 1967 [1931]. In *Hippocrates* IV (London: Loeb Editions, William Heinemann): pp. 496-7.
(3) "All things exist in all things, and all individuals in all individuals." Giovanni Pico della Mirandola (1463-1494). Quoted in S. A. Farmer, *Syncretism in the West: Pico's 900 Theses (1486): The Evolution of Traditional Religious and Philosophical Systems*, 1998 (Tempe, AZ: Medieval & Renaissance Tests & Studies): p. 195.
(4) Gerard Manley Hopkins. *The Journals and Papers of Gerard Manley Hopkins*, ed. Humphrey House, 1966 [1959] (Oxford: Oxford University Press): p. 230.
(5) Stéphane Mallarmé, the first line of 'Un coup de dés', 1897: "A throw of the dice will never abolish chance."

(6) William Wordsworth, *The Prelude*, 1805 text, Book II: 'School Time', ed. Ernest de Selincourt, 1969 [1933] (London: Oxford University Press): p. 31, lines 401-405.

(7) Carl Gustav Jung: 'Vorwort zum I Ging', in *Zur Psychologie westlicher und östlicher Religion* (*Gesammelte Werke* 11), 1963 (Zürich: Rascher Verlag): p. 641, para. 976. The literal translation is: "so the idea came to me to imagine the book as if it were a person and to put the question to it." R. F. C. Hull, Jung's principal translator, renders this very loosely as: "Why not venture a dialogue with a book that purports to be animated?" See 'Foreword', *I Ching or Book of Changes*, the Wilhelm/ Baynes version, 1965 (London: Routledge & Kegan Paul): p. xxvi. See also C. G. Jung, *Psychology and Religion: West and East* (*Collected Works*, Vol. 11), 2001 [1958] (Hove: Routledge): p. 594, para. 976.

(8) "[C]haque langue forme un système ou tout se tient." ["Every language forms a system where everything holds together," i.e. "in which everything coheres."] Antoine Meillet, *Introduction à l'étude comparative des langues indo-européennes* 1903 (Paris: Hachette): p. 407.

(9) George Seferis: a line from his poem 'Στα περιχώρα της Κερήνειας' ('In the Kyrenia District'). It has two English interpretations: "This isn't our world, it's Homer's" and "These aren't our people, they're Homer's." See George Seferis, *Collected Poems 1924-1955*, trs. Edmund Keeley and Philip Sherrard (London: Jonathan Cape. 1969): pp. 466-467.

(10) Ezra Pound, *Drafts and Fragments of Cantos CX-CXVII*, 1970. (London: Faber and Faber): p. 27.

pp. 3-21, 'Initiating' and 'Responding, Corresponding'

The poem-sequences devoted to the first and second hexagrams contain an extra poem, in keeping with Chinese versions of the *I Ching* and *Zhouyi*. Hexagram 1 contains an extra reading for a divination in which all six solid *yang* lines change to broken *yin* lines (i.e. when *Qian* changes to *Kun*). Similarly, hexagram 2 contains an extra reading for the opposite situation (i.e. when *Qian* changes to *Kun*). For a good explanation, see Richard Rutt, *The Book Of Changes (Zhouyi): a Bronze Age Document*, 2002 [1996] (Richmond: Curzon): pp. 130-131.

The poems devoted to the first hexagram are influenced by Edward L. Shaughnessy's essay, '"Qian" and "Kun" Hexagrams', in his *Before Confucius, Studies in the Creation of the Chinese Classics*, 1997 (New York, NY: State University of New York Press): pp. 197-221. By means of a brilliant heuristic leap, Shaughnessy has interpreted the first two hexagrams as part of an astronomical clock, with the change-lines positioning the varying seasonal positions of the 'Dragon' constellation between spring and autumn.

p. 4, 'Heaven'

For Bent Nielsen. The phrase containing the four Chinese words in the base-line, 元亨利贞 *yuan heng li zhen,* appears as the 'head statement' for auguries (divinations) in six hexagrams in the *I Ching* (numbers 1, 2, 3, 17, 19 and 25). As one of a number of formulaic phrases in the *I Ching*, this has a strongly positive meaning: it indicates a fortunate and favourable interpretation of the outcome by the augurer. The English translation usually adopted is something like 'most auspicious', 'highly favourable', 'it furthers', 'it is favourable to divine', etc. Evidently, each of these ancient words is richly polysemic. The four characters 元亨利贞 came to be known as 'the four qualities' or 'the four virtues', with various other correlating contexts such as the elements, the cardinal directions and the seasons. For the last of these, see also the companion poem 'Earth', p. 14 and the note to it on p. 536 below.

p. 6, 'What Zhang Zai thought'

For Steve Spence. Zhang Zai (1020–1077 CE) was a philosopher and astronomer. For lines 10-13, see Ira E. Kasoff, *The Thought of Chang Tsai*, 1984 (Cambridge: Cambridge University Press): p. 64. See also the companion poems, 'What Zhang Zai said', p. 444, and 'What Zhang Zai knew', p. 446.

p. 7, 'Cohering, inhering'

In memory of David Bohm (1917–1992). The last stanza embeds oblique references to lines by Wallace Stevens ("Oh! Blessed rage for order, pale Ramon") and Ezra Pound ("i.e. it coheres all right"). See Stevens's 'The Idea of Order at Key West', *Collected Poetry and Prose*, eds. Frank Kermode and Joan Richardson, 1997 (Library of America): p. 106. And for Pound see his 'Canto CXVI', *Drafts and Fragments of Cantos CX-CXVII*, 1970 (London: Faber and Faber): p. 27.

p. 9, 'Absolute'

For Chen Shangzhen.

p. 10, 'Light fills and fails'

In memory of Sebastian Barker (1945–2014). See also the companion villanelle, 'The force that fills and empties', p. 20.

p. 11, '☯ *Supreme Ultimate*'

For Lee Moden. The title is a translation of the Chinese phrase *taiji,* which is represented symbolically as ☯. Known in the West as the 'yin-yang symbol', in Chinese this is called *taijitu*, lit. 'diagram of the Supreme Ultimate'. This name is the basis of the martial arts discipline *taijiquan* ('*taiji* fist'). Shen Jin has described this fist as "so large that nothing could be outside it and so small that nothing could be inside it" (*daoyin* workshop, Bristol, 26 July 2014). See also the note on p. 540 below to 'HARMONISING, PROSPERING', pp. 87-94.

p. 14, 'Earth'
For Bent Nielsen. In addition to many other layers of meaning based on what Sinologists and others usually call 'correlative thinking', the four words 元 *yuan*, 亨 *heng*, 利 *li*, and 贞 *zhen* may be used to designate the four seasons. See also the note on p. 535 above for the companion poem 'Heaven', p. 4.

p. 16, 'Walking, in a garden'
For David McMullen's garden in Grantchester.

p. 17, 'Change'
For Richard J. Smith. See also 'What the book said about itself', p. 160.

p. 19, 'A yellow lower garment'
For Lara Burns and David, Imogen and Alex Lightning. Lines 14-16 echo and respond to Ezra Pound's plaints and confessions: 'I cannot make it cohere', 'I cannot make it flow thru', and 'it coheres all right / even if my notes do not cohere'. See 'Canto XCVI', *Drafts and Fragments of Cantos CX-CXVII*, 1970 (London: Faber and Faber): pp. 26-27. The base-line, *can'st 'ou see with the eyes of turquoise*, quotes 'Canto CX' (*ibid.*): p. 8. See also the tenth epigraph to this book; and 'Brightness diffusing', p. 518, lines 14-15. The second stanza here contains an oblique echo of William Blake's poem 'Jerusalem': "And did the Countenance Divine/ Shine forth upon our clouded hills?" See *The Poetry and Prose of William Blake*, ed. Geoffrey Keynes, 1956 (London: The Nonesuch Library): p. 375.

p. 20, 'The force that fills and empties'
In memory of Sebastian Barker (1945–2014). See also the companion villanelle, 'Light fills and fails', p. 10, and the final poem in this book, 'Brightness, diffusing', p. 518.

p. 21, 'Being simple'
For Sean Rys, and in memory of Octavio Paz (1914–1998). The character in the base-line 朴 (*pu*) means 'simple, plain, unadorned' or

'simplicity, plainness'. The word, which has many further overtones and shades of meaning in Daoism, is often translated as the 'uncut wood, unhewn block, uncarved log', etc., indicating the condition of pure potentiality.

p. 24, *'Seed, seeding, seedling'*
For Rupert Sheldrake. The base-line quotes the second line of William Blake's poem 'Auguries of Innocence'. See *The Poetry and Prose of William Blake*, ed. Geoffrey Keynes, 1956 (London: The Nonesuch Library): p. 118. See also the companion poem, 'Way, road, creode', on p. 202 and the note to it on p. 546.

p. 28, 'Street urchin, dancing'
Based on a dream.

p. 30, 'Biding (his) time'
For Paschalis Nikolaou.

p. 32, 'Child, counting'
To honour Marie-Louise von Franz (1915–1998). Modelled on a Yoruban chant quoted in her book *Number and Time*, tr. Andrea Dykes, 1974 (London: Rider & Company): p. 217. Franz cites her source as B. Maupoil, *La géomancie à l'ancienne côte des esclaves* (Paris, 1943): p. 529. See the companion pieces: 'Child, calculating', p. 37, and 'Father, counting', p. 457; and also 'Numbers exist but do not', p. 164, and the note on p. 544.

p. 34, 'In the primary school'
For Mick Gowar.

p. 35, 'Dependence, veiled'
Modelled on the interpretation of the third change-line given by Wang Bi (226–249 CE). See *The Classic of Changes*, tr. Richard John Lynn (New York, NY: Columbia University Press, 1994): pp. 161-162. For other poems influenced by Wang Bi's interpretations, see 'Across hill country', p. 142, 'Pierced like a laser', p. 322, and 'Relief, release', p. 325.

p. 37, 'Child, calculating'
See the companion pieces: 'Child, counting', p. 32, and the note to it above, and also 'Father, counting', p. 457, and the note to it on p. 560.

p. 38, 'Samuel Brighteyes'
Based on a dream.

p. 42, 'In the desert (1)'

See also the companion pieces, 'In the desert (2)', p. 85 and 'In the desert (3)', p. 242.

p. 46, 'Transparencies'
For Nasos Vayenas.

p. 48. 'Judge and jury'

Base-line: the many meanings of the word 中 (*zhong*) include 'centre, middle, inner, within, among, between, China, Chinese, to hit (the mark), to suffer, to win'. Most of these are integrally related: the character's form, a vertical line through a square, in itself pictures centrality. See also 'The ringing, *zhong*, the centre', p. 420, and the note to that poem on p. 558. The character occurs again in 中孚, INNER TRUSTING, p. 487; and see the next note too.

p. 53, 'A treaty'

中道(*zhong dao*) means 'the central path, the middle way'. This motif recurs on pp. 74, 82, 83, 90 and 258.

p. 54, 'A white horse'

A well-known story about sophistry told in the *Han Feizi* and many other Chinese texts. Han Fei lived c. 280–233 BC. See references in: R. P. Peerenboom, *Law and Morality in Ancient China: the Silk Manuscripts of Huang Lao* 1993 (Albany, NY: State University of New York Press): pp. 147-148; A. C. Graham, *Disputers of the Tao: Philosophical Argument in Ancient China*, 1989 (Chicago and La Salle, IL: Open Court Publishing Company): pp. 82-90; and Mark Edward Lewis, *Writing and Authority in Early China*, 1999 (Albany, NY: State University of New York Press): p. 33.

p. 56, 'Don't waste time'

In memory of Göran Printz-Påhlson (1931–2006). The finest sung versions of the 'Ballad of Joe Hill' are by Woody Guthrie, Paul Robeson and Joan Baez. For Robeson's version, see online at: http://www.youtube.com/watch?v=n8Kxq9uFDes. Reconsulted, 31 December, 2015.

p. 57, 'James Gibson remembers D Day'

Based on a report in *The Guardian*, '60 years Later', June 2, 2004. See online at: http://www.guardian.co.uk/uk/2004/jun/02/secondworldwar.world3. Reconsulted, September 11, 2015.

p. 58, 'In the spirit of Walt Whitman'
For Paul Scott Derrick.

pp. 59 and 60, 'Emperor's army, freed' and 'Emperor's army, captured'.
Based on the huge 'terracotta army' buried with Emperor Qin Shi
Huang in 210–209 BC, in Shaanxi province, discovered by local far-
mers in 1974.

pp. 63-70, 'ACCORDING, BINDING'
The dialogues in this cluster are inspired by the *Zhuangzi* (*Chuan-tzu*).
The versions I have relied on are *Chuang Tzu: Basic Writings*, tr. Burton
Watson, 1964 (New York, NY: Columbia University Press); *Chuang
Tsu, Inner Chapters*, trs. Gia-Fu Feng and Jane English, 1974 (London:
Wildwood House); and The *Book of Chuang Tzu*, trs. Martin Palmer, *et
al.*, 2006 [1996] (London and New York: Penguin Books).

pp. 64, 73, and 80, '*Listening to Schubert*', 'Green and red' and 'Water in the
stone jug'
For Melanie Rein.

p. 68, 'Still'
For Alan Hext. See Laozi (Lao Tsu), *Dao De Jing* (*Tao Te Ching*),
chapter 42. The translations I have relied on are by Gia-Fu Feng and
Jane English, *Tao Te Ching* (New York, NY: Vintage Books, 1972)
not paginated; and by Thomas Cleary, in *The Essential Tao*, 1991 (San
Francisco, CA: Harper Collins): p. 35. See also 'Numbers exist but do
not': p. 164.

p. 69, 'Ways and Whys'
For Yu Mingquan. See the companion poem 'Way Why One', p. 165.

p. 70, 'Things'
For Edward Luper.

p. 74, 'The nonplussed pleasures of love'
For 中道 (*zhong dao*) in the base-line: see the note above on p. 538 to 'A
Treaty', p. 53.

p. 76, 'Night, curtains open'
Base-line: *then fancies fly away … he'll fear not what men say*: lines from
'The Pilgrim' by John Bunyan in *Pilgrim's Progress*, Part 2. See also the
base-lines for 'Constancy' p. 91, and 'The poisoner', p. 381.

p. 81, 'Spread white rushes'
For Alastair Reid.

p. 82, 'What the tinker said (1)'
See also the companion piece, 'What the tinker said (2)', p. 429. For 中道 (*zhong dao*) in the base-line, see the note on p. 538 to 'A Treaty', p. 53.

p. 83, 'A shimmer of leaves'
For 中道 (*zhong dao*) in the base-line, see the previous note.

p. 85, 'In the desert (2)
For Mohammed Bennis. Line 14: *Al-Qamar*, 'the moon', Arabic. See also the companion pieces, 'In the desert (1)', p. 42, and 'In the desert (3)', p. 242.

p. 86, 'Poem for Daphne'
In memory of Daphne Dorrell (1919–2010).

pp. 87-94, 'Harmonising, Prospering'
No single English word can quite encapsulate the rich polysemy of the word 泰 *tai*, which is this hexagram's title in Chinese. The English translation conventionally given is 'peace' or 'tranquillity'. But this Chinese word also has a range of superlative and intensifying meanings that includes 'most', 'grand, great, greatness', 'safe', etc. Alfred Huang writes:

> Tai is one of the most auspicious words in the Chinese language. Originally it meant 'more than' or 'most'. It generally indicates a condition of being more than great (*The Complete I Ching*, Rochester, VT: Inner Traditions, 2004: p. 117).

What is more, the homophone *tai* 太 is an intensifier, meaning 'highest; greatest, utmost; too, too much; very; extreme, extremely', etc., as in the word *taiji* 太极. See the note on pp. 536-7 above on 'Supreme Ultimate', p. 11. Shaughnessy translates *tai* as 'Greatness' (*I Ching, the Classic of Changes, The Mawangdui Texts*, 1996: p. 105), and Richard Rutt as 'great' (*Zhouyi, the Book of Changes*, 2002 [1996]: p. 234). In order to make sense both of *tai* 泰 and of the trigram-configuration here, which is Earth (*Kun*) 'set above' or 'sitting on' or 'in' Heaven (*Qian*), my title 'Harmonising, Prospering' is intended to capture at least something of both these imagems.

p. 88, '*In King's College Chapel*'
For Stefano Maria Casella.

p. 90, 'Embracing the waste land'

The Shang dynasty ruled from around 1600 to around 1050 BCE. This poem owes a good deal to Alfred Huang's reading of the second change-line. See *The Complete I Ching*, 2004, (Rochester, VT: Inner Traditions): pp. 119-121. For 中道 (*zhong dao*) in the base-line, see the note on p. 538 to 'A Treaty', p. 53. For other poems connected to Huang, see pp. 366 and 389.

p. 91, 'Constancy'

In memory of Frank Kermode (1919–2010). The base-line quotes lines from 'The Pilgrim' by John Bunyan in *Pilgrim's Progress*, Part 2. This hymn was sung at the memorial service for Frank Kermode in King's College Chapel, Cambridge, on 7 May 2011. See also the base-lines for 'Night, curtains open', p. 76, and 'The Poisoner', p. 381.

p. 93, 'Working for Laban'

For Melanie Rein. For this part of the story of Jacob, Leah and Rachel, see *Genesis* 29: 9-28.

p. 102, ' A sacrifice'

Homage to Maksymilian Kolbe (1894–1941), a Polish Franciscan friar murdered by the Nazis in Auschwitz after volunteering to die in place of a stranger, Franz Gajowniczek (1901–1995). Kolbe was canonised in 1982.

p. 106, 'Ventura Street'

See also the complementary poem, 'Language palazzo', p. 188.

p. 112, 'Order in grand design'

For Jeremy Hooker.

p. 114, 'Ground'

For Robert Hass.

p. 117, 'Dark gates of things'

For Elaine Feinstein.

p. 120, 'Way'

For Wang Bang. The word 道 (*dao*) means 'way, path, road'. This motif recurs singly on pp. 160, 256, 340, and 452, and in combination with 中 (*zhong*) on pp. 74, 82, 83, 90, and 258. See also the note on p. 550 to 'Holding Fast' p. 266.

p. 121, 'Getting down in'

For Theo Breuer.

p. 122, 'We wash things'
For Angela Leighton.

p. 123, 'She sweeps shadows'
For Antoinette Moses.

p. 128, '*Somewhere to go*'
For Arijana Mišić-Burns.

p. 129, 'Stargate One is open'
For Joy Hendry.

p. 130, 'Go here'
For Imogen Lightning. The base line echoes Buddy Holly's song 'Not Fade Away'.

p. 132, '*Beli andjeo*'
In memory of Ivan V. Lalić (1931–1996). The title, in Serbian, means 'White Angel', which is the popular name for the fresco 'The Angel at Christ's Tomb' in Mileševa Monastery, Serbia. Mileševa was founded by King Vladislav in the 13th century. See also RB, *Under Balkan Light*, 2011 (Exeter: Shearsman Books): esp. the cover, and pp. 34-35, 52-55, and 92).

p. 133, 'She wrote herself into Death'
Homage to the philosopher Gillian Rose (1947–1995). The poem is based on a mental image that I had stored – according to which Gillian Rose had decided to hold a pen in her hand as she lay dying, and that she kept on writing until death took her. Her writing trailed away, unfinished, into a scrawl. This composite visual image was so clear that I believed for several years that I had first read about it as a historically true event. I was convinced that I had seen a facsimile photo of this last incomplete piece of her writing, accompanying the printed text. As it turned out, no such photo exists, and I must have dreamed or imagined it. However, thanks to my wife Melanie Rein, much later, and to my great astonishment, I came across Gillian Rose's last notes, edited by Howard Caygill. These bore a striking, even uncanny resemblance to my earlier fantasy. See Caygill's 'The Final Notebooks of Gillian Rose', *Women, a cultural review*, 9:1, 1998: pp. 6-18.

pp. 135-142, 'FOLLOWING'
For Lin Xueqing.

p. 138, 'Other voices'

Homage to George Herbert (1593–1633). The last three lines echo his poem 'Life'.

p. 139, 'A thing like this'

For Norman Jope.

p. 141, 'You'

In memory of Edmond Jabès (1912–1991). The last lines refer to RB's *Book With No Back Cover*, 2003 (London: David Paul).

p. 142, 'Across hill country'

Widely diverging interpretations of the top line of hexagram 17 are offered by Richard Wilhelm, Alfred Huang, and other modern commentators and translators. Here, as in several other instances, I follow Wang Bi (226–249 CE). See *The Classic of Changes*, tr. Richard John Lynn, 1994 (New York, NY: Columbia University Press): p. 246. See also the companion piece, 'To protect the kingdom', p. 372. For other poems influenced by Wang Bi's interpretations, see 'Dependence veiled', p. 35, 'Pierced like a laser', p. 322, and 'Relief, release', p. 325.

p. 150, 'Recluse, autumn morning'.

For Richard J. Smith.

p. 152, '*Young Arthur*'

In memory of John Heath-Stubbs (1918–2006). See also the companion pieces, 'The end of Arthur', p. 157, and 'Merlin to young Arthur', p. 507.

p. 157, 'The end of Arthur'

For Kim Landers. This poem is taken almost straight out of the *Morte d'Arthur*. See Sir Thomas Malory, *Works*, ed. Eugène Vinaver, 1983 [1971] (Oxford: Oxford University Press): pp. 714-717. See also the companion pieces, 'Young Arthur', p. 152 and 'Merlin to young Arthur', p. 507.

p. 158, 'At Dragon Gate'

For Wang Liping. See the story of his training as a Daoist adept in *Opening the Dragon Gate: The Making of a Modern Taoist Wizard*, by Chen Kaiguo and Zheng Shunchao, tr. Thomas Cleary, 1998 (North Clarendon, VT: Tuttle Publishing). See also the companion poem, 'At Shipwreck Head', p. 491.

p. 160, '*What the book said about itself*'
For Richard J. Smith. See also p. 17, 'Change'. For 道 (*dao*) in the baseline, see the note on p. 541 to 'Way', p. 120.

p. 161, 'Patterns of our own'
For Edward L. Shaughnessy.

p. 162, 'First came number'
Lines 3-18 are condensed from Roy Harris, *The Origin of Writing* (London: Duckworth, 2002 [1980]): pp. 134-135.

p. 164, 'Numbers exist but do not'
Homage to Marie-Louise von Franz (1915–1998). Lines 9-18 are quoted directly from her book *Number and Time*, tr. Andrea Dykes, 1974 (London: Rider & Company): p. 166. See also the note on p. 537 above to 'Child counting', p. 32, and the note on p. 539 to 'Still', p. 68.

p. 165, 'Way Why One'
For Antonio Domínguez Rey. See the companion poem 'Ways and Whys', p. 69.

p. 166, 'Lines unbroken and broken'
For Kim Landers.

pp. 169 and 170, 'Across the bare langscape' and 'In his wake'
In memory of W. S. Graham (1918–1986). Lines 12-18 in the second poem echo a theme of Osip Mandelstam. See the essay 'To an Interlocutor' in his *Selected Essays*, 1977, tr. Sidney Monas (Austin, TX: University of Texas Press): pp. 58-64, esp. pp. 59-60.

p. 177, 'Leaf. Leaf.'
For Jesper Svenbro.

p. 178, 'Coolly calling'
For Melanie Rein.

p. 179, 'Concerning light and her'
For Kim Landers.

pp. 180 & 182, 'When she sang in the bazaar' and 'When she sang in the white alley'.
These poems form a pair. Several years after writing them, I discovered the story of Erh, a woman of Han, who sang in exchange for a meal: "When she left, her lingering notes curled round the beams of the gate and did not die away for three days; the bystanders thought that she was

still there." *The Book of Lieh-Tzu*, tr. A. C. Graham, 1991 [1961], p. 109 (London: Mandala, Harper-Collins).

p. 181, 'Now'
The earliest-written poem in this book, first drafted in 1972–3. See also the note on p. 561 below for '*Two lakes, joined*', p. 464.

p. 185, 'We thank our Führer'
Line 6: Kurt Schuschnigg (1897–1977) was the Austrian Chancellor in 1938. He opposed Germany's annexation (*Anschluss*) of his country in that year and was imprisoned by the Nazis until the end of the Second World War, first in solitary confinement, then in the concentration camps of Sachsenhausen and Dachau.

p. 186, 'The forensic archaeologist's testimony'
In memory of Annonciata Mukandoli (1976–2004). Based on 'The butterfly hunter', an account of the 1994 massacre in Rwanda by Margaret Cox, *The Independent Magazine*, 18 July 2004. See online at http://www.independent.co.uk/news/world/africa/the-butterfly-hunter-6165327.html. See also Sean Motl, 'Nyamata Memorial Church Visit', posted August 29, 2012, online at http://turikumwe.wordpress.com /2012/08/29nyamata-memorial-church-visit. Both reconsulted, July 25, 2015.

p. 187, 'After the massacre'.
Line 17: the *hamsah*, from Arabic *khomsah*, meaning 'five', is a geometrically stylised amulet depicting the palm of the right hand with an eye in its centre. This eye is usually blue or blue-green. Made of enamel, porcelain, precious or semi-precious stones, or metals, it is worn or carried, or placed near the entrance of a house, to ward off the Evil Eye. It is widely used in the Arab world and in Israel. See also 'Words for a *hamsah*', p. 253.

p. 188, 'Language Palazzo'
See also the complementary poem, 'Ventura Street', p. 106.

p. 190, '(A) coherent language'
For Michael Heller. תיקון: the Hebrew word *tikkun*, meaning 'mending, restoration, restitution', is a fertile and resonant term in Kabbalistic thought. See Gershom Scholem, *Major Trends in Jewish Mysticism* (London: Thames and Hudson): pp. 273-278, esp. p. 275: "The task of man is seen to consist in the direction of his whole inner purpose towards the restoration of the original harmony which was

disturbed by the original defect – the Breaking of the Vessels – and those powers of evil and sin which date from that time." See also '*Tikkun*, Majdanek', p. 294, and the note on p. 551 below.

p. 192, '*Everyone knows the ways*'
For Clive Wilmer.

pp. 193 and 194, 'Home east' and 'Both ways meant exile'
For Michael Rutschky.

p. 195, 'With her own old key'
For Jasna Levinger-Goy.

p. 197, 'Under the bridge'
For Jelena Vojvodić and Yiram and Elian Aldouby.

p. 198, 'I know a house'
In memory of Alan Clodd (1918–2002).

p. 200, '*Only breathe in corners*'
For Imogen Lightning.

p. 201, 'A singer from County Clare'
For Gabriel Rosenstock.

p. 202, 'Way, road, creode'
For Rupert Sheldrake. 'Creode' is a word coined by the biologist C. H. Waddington (1905–1975), from Greek χρή [*chri*] ('necessary') and ὁδος [*odos*] ('path, way, road'). Waddington deploys it to signify "a path of change which is determined by the initial conditions of a system and which once entered upon cannot be abandoned". See *The Nature of Life*, 1961 (London: George Allen & Unwin): p. 64. Waddington's concept was taken up by Rupert Sheldrake as a way of grounding and modelling his theory of morphic resonance. See *The Presence of the Past: Morphic Resonance and the Habits of Nature*, 2011 (London: Icon Books): esp. pp. 205-211. See also the companion poem, '*Seed, seeding, seedling*', p. 24 and the note to it on p. 537.

p. 203, 'A twist'
For Chee Lay Tan.

p. 205, 'Alexander calling'
For Alex Lightning.

p. 206, 'Clown'
For Adam Darius.

p. 208, '*Cox's Pippin*'
In memory of Alexis Burns (1947–2015).

p. 209, 'Thesaurus'
Line 16: the word "pleasures" could equally well be replaced by "treasures", which is cognate with the title. For the base-line, "put aside your spiritual tortoise": see also Liu An, King of Huainan, *The Huainanzi* [139 BCE], trs. John S. Major *et al.*, 2010 (New York, NY: Columbia University Press): pp. 613, 628-9, and 644.

p. 210, 'Still and on'
For Silvia Pio.

p. 211, 'A maze book'
Line 9: '*kinging*' is a term back-translated from the modern Greek verb βασιλεύει [*vasilevi*], which literally means 'is reigning', 'is in kingship', from the word βασιλεύς [*vasilefs*], 'king'. It is ascribed to the sun and designates the sun setting, i.e. 'the sun in his majesty'. See also the first line of 'Volta' in RB, *For the Living, Selected Longer Poems, 1965-2000*, 2011 (Exeter: Shearsman Books): p. 157; and see also 'Volta: A Multilingual Anthology', *The International Literary Quarterly*, online at http://interlitq.org/issue9/volta/job.php. Reconsulted, June 4, 2015.

p. 212, 'Behind the bean stalks'
For Gully Burns.

p. 213, 'Jade cup'
In memory of Joseph Needham (1900–1995). Lines 1-7 are taken from his *Science and Civilisation in China*, vol. 1, 1954, (Cambridge: Cambridge University Press): p. 41.

p. 214, 'Ground, grounds, store'
In memory of Lev Vygotsky (1896–1934) and Roman Jakobson (1896–1982). See also the companion poems: 'Roots, roofs, routes', p. 369; 'Lungfish', p. 370; and 'This now', p. 373.

p. 216, '*Summer, svemir*'
In Serbian and Croatian, *svemir* means 'universe, space'. Derived from Old Slavonic, the word is constructed from two parts, *sve* ('all') and *mir* (мир 'world', 'universe'. 'community'). The conflation of the homophone *mir*, meaning 'peace, calm, tranquillity, creates an interesting ambiguity. Hence the modern word *svemir* simultaneously suggests not only 'entire world' but also 'all-encompassing peace, complete tranquillity'. In Russian, prior to reforms of orthography in 1918, there

was no ambiguity, as the spellings of the two words were distinct: миръ ('peace') and міръ ('the universe').

p. 219, 'Oh my (our) country'
Lines 7 and 8 echo the first line of William Blake's poem 'London' in *Songs of Experience*: "I wander thro' each charter'd street." See *The Poetry and Prose of William Blake*, ed. Geoffrey Keynes, 1956 (London: The Nonesuch Library): p. 75.

p. 221, 'Wild strawberry'
For Jelena Vojvodić.

p. 222, 'Apple'
In memory of Staniša Brkić (1950–2013) and Slobodan Pavićević (1942–2013), friends who both lived in Kragujevac, Central Serbia. Based on a dream.

p. 225, 'Building a tabernacle'
In memory of Rabbi Werner Van der Zyl (1902–1984).

p. 227, 'The minister has been tainted'
See also RB, *The Manager* (Exeter: Shearsman Books) 2011: p. 115.

p. 229, 'Letter from Court'
Line 15: Count Andrey Petrovich Shuvalov (1743–1789) was Chamberlain to Empress Catherine II of Russia.

pp. 231-238, 'FALLING (IN A PIT)'
Homage to the three brothers, Ali, Bayazid and Midhat Bourequat. Based on the documentary film *On the Dignity of the Human Soul: Ali Bourequat and his imprisonment in Tazmamart*, directed by Ingela Romare, Ö. Rönneholmesvägen 4, SE-211 47 Malmö, 1996.

p. 240, '*Over whole skies*'
For Catherine Pickstock.

p. 241, 'Dust speck'
For Shi Dao.

p. 242, 'In the desert' (3)
For Mohammed Bennis. See also the companion pieces, 'In the desert (1)', p. 42, and 'In the desert (2)', p. 85.

p. 243, 'Indelible shadows, tattooed'
Base-line: *Sonnenuntergangstraurigkeit* means 'sunset melancholy'. See also RB, *Book With No Back Cover*, 2003 (London: David Paul): p. 38.

p. 244, 'Towards my window'
For Joanne Limburg.

p. 245, 'Untouchable light, miraculous air'
For Anthony Davies. The base-line echoes John Donne's poem 'A Valediction: Forbidding Mourning'.

p. 246, 'No horizon at Trabzen'
For Michael Duffett.

p. 248, 'A lake on a mountain'
For Jidi Majia. In June 2016, I visited Lake Lugu on the borders of the provinces of Sichuan and Yunnan. This lake, which is in the centre of Ninglang Yi Autonomous County, is 2,600 metres above sea level. The area is inhabited by many minority ethnic groups, foremost among whom are the Nosuo and the Yi peoples. My journey to Lake Lugu occurred during the first Xichang Silk Road International Poetry Festival, organised by Jidi Majia, Chinese poet of Yi-Nosuo ancestry, and champion of these minority cultures.

p. 253, 'Words for a *hamsah*'
For *hamsah*, see the note on p. 545 to 'After the massacre', p. 187.

p. 256, '*Between is and not*'
For 道 (*dao*) in the base-line, see the note on p. 541 to 'Way', p. 120.

p. 257. 'Working at it'
For Geneviève Guetemme.

p. 258, 'The way you chose'
For 中道 (*zhong dao*) in the base-line, see the note on p. 538 to 'A Treaty', p. 53.

p. 260, 'Who list to hunt'
The title repeats the first line of a sonnet by Thomas Wyatt. The base-line comes from the same poem. See: *The Complete Poems of Sir Thomas Wyatt*, ed. R. A. Rebholz (London: Penguin Books, 1997 [1978]): p. 77.

p. 261, 'Field Work'
In memory of Barrie Irving (1942–2013) and for Patricia Carloss-Irving.

p. 264, '*Moses*'
Base-line: *get thee up … into the high mountains*: Isaiah 40:9; and the alto chorus 'O Thou That Tellest Good Tidings to Zion' in Handel's *Messiah*.

p. 266, 'Holding fast'

In memory of Ueshiba Morihei (1883–1969), founder of Aikido 合気道 (lit. the 'way of unifying life-energy'). The Japanese word *ki* 気 is cognate with Chinese *qi* 氣 or 气, ('life-energy', 'vital breath'). The Japanese word *do* 道 is cognate with Chinese *dao* 道, 'way': see also the note on p. 541 to 'Way', p. 120.

p. 268, 'Split off'

Based on a dream.

p. 269, 'Retreating'

In memory of Xiao Yao, who died in 1985, aged about 96; and for Robert Peng. For Xiao Yao's biography, see Robert Peng, *Qigong Master, My Life and Secret Teachings*, written with Rafael Nasser, 2010 (New York, NY: Rainbow Tree Publishing): esp. 'The Mysterious Mr. Tan', pp. 9-19 and 21-85. For the companion piece, see ''Shedding', p. 397, and the note on p. 556.

p. 270, 'In Epping Forest'

For Shi Jing.

p. 272, '*Tree*'

For Wang Ying. See the companion poem, 'Strengths', p. 345, and also the chant poem of the same title in RB, *For the Living, Selected Poems 1965–2000* (Exeter: Shearsman Books): pp. 117-130.

p. 276, 'Levers behind the panel'

Homage to Mikis Theodorakis. Lines 4-5 are translated from 'Nous sommes deux' ('Είμαστε δυό' [There are two of us]), a song from his cycle *Chansons pour Andréas* [Songs for Andreas] (Polydor 239302), composed April-June 1968, and dedicated to his fellow-prisoner Andreas Lentakis.

p. 277, 'Thirty-six just men'

For Stephen Wilson. The legend of the *Tzadikim Nistarim*, 'hidden righteous ones', or *Lamed Vav Tzadikim*, 'thirty-six righteous ones', is rooted in the mystical traditions of Judaism. The idea is that at any one time, thirty-six human beings walk the earth whose task is to care for humanity and guard the Divine Presence. Unknown to one another, and with roles unknown even to themselves, they embody humility. When one dies, another is born.

p. 280, '*At an oblique angle*'

For Lucy Hamilton.

p. 281, 'Dawn'
In memory of Roberto Sanesi (1930–2001). Lines 11-12 provide the title for the anthology *Light Unlocked*, ed. K. Crossley-Holland, 2005 (London: Enitharmon Press). See also the companion poem, 'Early morning', p. 368.

p. 283, 'Light and things'
In memory of Renos Loizou (1948–2013).

p. 284, 'Morning, open windows'
For Melanie Rein.

p. 285, 'Dawn will come and have your eyes'
The title and first two lines responds to Cesare Pavese's poem 'Verrà la morte e avrà i tuoi occhi' ('Death will come and have your eyes'). See Cesare Pavese, *Poesie*, 1961 (Turin: Giulio Einaudi): p. 165. For RB's translation, see *The Southern Review* 5[1], Winter 1969: pp. 98-99.

p. 286, 'Winter solstice'
In memory of Leon Kuhn (1954–2013). Last line: eggs of a light blue colour are laid naturally by several breeds of chicken, including the Old Cotswold Legbar.

pp. 288 and 294, '*Meditation at Majdanek*' and '*Tikkun*, Majdanek'
Majdanek was a Nazi concentration camp, Lublin, Poland.

p. 290, 'Under occupation'
Homage to Oscar Schindler (1908–1974).

p. 293, "To write a poem after Auschwitz is barbaric"
Reply to Theodore Adorno (1903–1969). The statement quoted in the title appeared in his essay 'Cultural Criticism and Society,' in *Prisms*, trs. Samuel and Sherry Weber, 1967 (Cambridge, MA: MIT Press): p. 19.

p. 294, '*Tikkun*, Majdanek'
Homage to Gershom Scholem (1897–1982) and Walter Benjamin (1892–1940). See *The Correspondence of Walter Benjamin and Gershom Scholem, 1932-1940*, trs. Gary Smith and Andre Lefevre, 1992 (Cambridge, MA: Harvard University Press). See also '(A) coherent language', p. 190; and for an explanation of the word *Tikkun*, see the note to that poem on pp. 545-6. Here, the word appears in Hebrew in the base-line: תיקון.

p. 296, '*Home*'
For Lara Burns.

p. 297, 'Lara's garden in August'
For Lara Burns, Jelena Vojvodić and Arijana Mišić-Burns.

p. 298, 'Ownership'
Homage to Jacques Derrida (1930–2004).

p. 299, 'Hospitality'
For Robert Lee.

p. 300, 'Poverty'
In memory of Harry Stamper (d. 2012).

p. 301, 'Necessity'
For Will Hill.

p. 302, 'Small poem for Gully'
For Gully Burns.

p. 309, 'The stone carver'
For Rosie Musgrave. For her website, see online at http://www.
rosiemusgrave.com/. Reconsulted, November 15, 2015.

p. 316, 'Becket'
Thomas à Becket, born c. 1118, Chancellor to King Henry II of
England, and later Archbishop of Canterbury. Murdered in 1170.

p. 318, 'Theseus at Colonus'
'The Underworld's Queen': Persephone. See Theseus's last speech in
Sophocles, *Oedipus at Colonus*.

p. 321, 'Graduating'
For Arijana Mišić-Burns.

p. 322, 'Pierce like a laser'
The last lines derive from the interpretation given to the second change-
line by Wang Bi (226–249 CE) in *The Classic of Changes*, tr. Richard
John Lynn, 1994 (New York, NY: Columbia University Press): pp.
382-383. For other poems influenced by Wang Bi's interpretations, see
'Dependence, veiled', p. 35, 'Across hill country', p. 142, and 'Relief,
release', p. 325.

p. 325, 'Relief, release'
Content derives from the interpretation given to the fifth change-line by
Wang Bi (226–249 CE), (*ibid.*): p. 384. For other poems influenced by
Wang Bi's interpretations, see 'Dependence, veiled', p. 35, 'Across hill
country', p. 142, and 'Pierce like a laser', p. 322.

p. 330, 'Before you go'

In the last three lines, plural imperatives for the verb 'work' appear in French, German, Serbian/Bosnian/Croatian, Italian and Greek. The final Chinese character *gong* 工 means 'work, practice, cultivation'. The graph appears in words for several martial arts, e.g. *qigong* 气功 and *gongfu* or *kung fu* 功夫. In these disciplines, as in meditation, the art of 'working' consists, paradoxically and precisely, in non-action. In the base-line, the term 无为 (*wu wei*) means 'without doing, without action', and 'without being, without becoming'. This key concept in Daoism, which is reflected in Chinese, Japanese and Korean martial arts, is also translated as 'effortless action'. See also: Approximations', p. 419; 'Nothing happens', p. 421; 'Ringing his bowl-bell', p. 422; and the notes to those poems on pp. 557-8.

p. 331, 'Clothèd all in green-o'

The title and line 5 derive from the English traditional song 'Green grow the rushes-o'.

p. 333, '*C'est la vie, mort de la Mort!*'

For Tony Frazer. The title comes from César Vallejo. See his *Complete Later Poems 1923–1938*, eds. & trs. Valentino Gianuzzi and Michael Smith, 2005 (Exeter: Shearsman Books): pp. 146-147. See also '*Del libro de la* naturaleza', p. 338, and '*Hoy le ha entrado una astilla*', p. 435. The last line, "Poetry is a criticsm of death," takes up Matthew Arnold's statement that poetry is "a criticism of life", in 'The Study of Poetry' (his introduction to *The English Poets*, ed. T. H. Ward, London, 1880). See his *Essays in Criticism* [Second Series], ed. S. R. Littlewood, 1960 (London: Macmillan): p. 3. For earlier instances of RB's reply, see *Manual*, 2014 (Bristol: Shearsman Books): p. 33; and 'A Little Further', in *Imagems I*, 2013 (Bristol: Shearsman Books): p. 10.

p. 334, 'The complete art of drowning'

For Lara Burns. This is the earliest poem in this book: its first draft was written in 1971. See also the note on p. 561 for '*Two lakes, joined*', p. 464.

p. 336, '*Sloop-building*'

For Paul Pines.

p. 338, '*Del libro de la naturaleza*'

The title and line 13 are from a poem by César Vallejo, *Complete Later Poems 1923-1938*, eds. & trs. Valentino Gianuzzi and Michael Smith,

2005 (Exeter: Shearsman Books): pp. 196-197. See also p. 333, *'C'est la vie, mort de la Mort!'*, and *'Hoy le ha entrado una astilla'*, p. 435.

p. 340, 'All I could ever'
For 道 (*dao*) in the base-line, see the note on p. 541 to 'Way', p. 120.

p. 341, These poems shred themselves'
For Norman Finkelstein.

p. 345, 'Strengths'
For Alastair Reid. The word 'strengths' is the longest syllable in the English language, containing eight phonemes. See also the companion piece, *'Tree'*, p. 272.

p. 349, 'Mist dispersing'
For Robert Archambeau.

pp. 351-358, 'COUPLING'
On the intertwined erotic images in hexagram 44, see S. J. Marshall, *The Mandate of Heaven: Hidden History in the I Ching*, 2001, chapter X, 'Melons, willows, hoarfrost, and creepers' (New York, NY: Columbia University Press): pp. 112-126.

p. 355, 'Danitsa'
Transliteration of 'Danica', the love-goddess and morning star in Serbian mythology and folklore. See RB, 'Do vidjenja Danitse', in *Under Balkan Light*, 2011 (Exeter: Shearsman Books): pp. 1-15; and the bilingual English-Serbian edition *Do vidjenja Danice*, 2011 (Belgrade and Kragujevac: Srpska književika Zadruga with City of Kragujevac).

p. 360, 'Midsummer Fair'
For Francesca and Angela Mansfield, and Lara and Gully Burns. The annual fair on Midsummer Common in Cambridge is one of the oldest in England.

p. 361, 'See, one by one they arrive'
For John Gery.

p. 364, 'Beautiful September morning'
For Melanie Rein.

p. 366, 'Celebrity'
This poem follows Alfred Huang's interpretation of the top change-line. See his *The Complete I Ching*, 2004 (Rochester, VT: Inner Traditions): pp. 365-366. For other poems influenced by Huang, see pp. 90 and 389.

p. 368, 'Early morning'

For Giuseppe Napolitano. See the companion poem, 'Dawn', p. 281.

p. 369, 'Roots, roofs, routes'

For Yorick Wilks. Inspired by Roman Jakobson's discussion of the pur-
posiveness inherent in biological and linguistic structures and processes.
See his *Main Trends in the Science of Language*, 1973 (London: George
Allen & Unwin): pp. 55-59. Embedded references to Jakobson's text
either quote, paraphrase or summarise statements by the following
biologists: lines 1-3, N. A Bernšteyn; lines 7-9, M. L. Cetlin, Jonas
Salk, C. S. Pittendrigh and J. Monod; and lines 13-15, J. Monod. The
base-line quotes 'Mythistorema 23' by George Seferis, in his *Collected
Poems 1924-1955*, trs. Edmund Keeley and Philip Sherrard (London:
Jonathan Cape): p. 58. See also the companion poems: 'Ground,
grounds, store', p. 214; 'Lungfish', p. 370; and 'This now', p. 373.

p. 370, 'Lungfish'

Lines 2 and 8: during the late Paleozoic and the early Mesozoic years,
between 300 and 200 million years ago, Panthalassa (from Greek παν
[*pan*] 'all', 'entire', and θάλασσα [*thalassa*] 'ocean') was the global ocean
that surrounded the supercontinent Pangaea (Γαῖα [*Gaia*] 'mother-
earth'). It included the Pacific Ocean to the west and north and the
Tethys Ocean to the southeast. See also the previous note.

p. 372, 'To protect the Kingdom'

For Yang Guohua. See also the companion piece, 'Across hill country',
p. 142.

p. 373, 'This now'

Homage to Lev Vygotsky (1896–1934) and Roman Jakobson (1896–
1982). See also the companion poems: 'Ground, grounds, store', p. 214;
'Roots, roofs, routes', p. 369; and 'Lungfish, p. 370.

pp. 374, 'Wall'

For Yang Guohua.

p. 381, 'Poisoner'

Base-line: '*whoso beset him round … do but themselves confound*': lines
from 'The Pilgrim' by John Bunyan in *Pilgrim's Progress*, Part 2. See also
the base-lines for 'Night, curtains open', p. 76, and 'Constancy', p. 91.

pp. 383-90, 'WELLING, REPLENISHING'

Homage to Carl Gustav Jung (1875–1961). Following his first
experiences of divining, Jung interpreted hexagram 50 (entitled 'The

Cauldron' in the Wilhelm/Baynes version) as the voice of the *I Ching* itself. See his 'Foreword' to *The I Ching or Book of Changes*, trs. Richard Wilhelm and Cary F. Baynes, 1965 [1951], pp. xxvi-xxviii (London: Routledge & Kegan Paul). My own preferred imagem for the *I Ching* itself is this hexagram 48, whose Chinese name 井 (*jing*) means 'well'. See also the discussion on the 'well-field' system, 井田 (*jing tian*) in the 'Postscript', p. 526.

p. 384, '*Consultation of the diagrams*'
In memory of John Blackwood (1943–1993) and for Kim Landers.

p. 386, 'Sometimes they answer'
Homage to John Blofeld (1913–1987). See his accounts of his first divinations in his book, *I Ching: The Book of Change*, 1991 (New York, NY: Penguin Arcana): esp. pp. 25-30.

p. 388, '*I Ching*'
In memory of Richard Wilhelm (1873–1930).

p. 389, 'I lower my question'
To honour Alfred Huang (b. 1921). For poems influenced by his interpretations of the *I Ching*, see pp. 90 and 366.

p. 393, 'The statues'
In memory of Miroslav Holub (1923–1998). The burghers of Calais: a sculpture by Auguste Rodin.

p. 397, 'Shedding'
In memory of Xiao Yao and for Robert Peng. The base-line quotes the first line of William Blake's poem 'The Tyger'. See *The Poetry and Prose of William Blake*, ed. Geoffrey Keynes, pp. 72 and 92, 1956 (London The Nonesuch Library). For the companion piece, see 'Retreating', p. 269, and the note on p. 550.

pp. 399-406, 'Cooking, Sacrificing'
Based on the story of Croesus in Herodotus, who consulted the Oracle of Delphi about his plans to go to war with Persia. (See *The History of Herodotus*, Book I, tr. George Rawlinson, online at http://classics.mit.edu/Herodotus/history.1.i.html. Reconsulted, July 23, 2015.) The turtle is common to both the Greek story and the early Chinese divinatory practice.

For the ancient Chinese use of oracles for counselling on military matters, see David N. Keightley, *The Ancestral Landscape: Time, Space, and Community in Late Shang China*, 2000 (Berkeley, CA: University of California at Berkeley, Institute of East Asian Studies): esp. pp. 66-72; and Richard J. Smith, *The I Ching: a Biography*, 2012 (Princeton, NJ: Princeton University Press): p. 110. For ancient doubts about the efficacy of oracles in military decision-making, see Mark Edward Lewis, *Writing and Authority in Early China*, 1999 (Albany, NY: State University of New York): p. 249 and p. 458 [note 30]; and Kidder Smith, '*Zhouyi* Interpretation from Accounts in the *Zuochan*' (*Harvard Journal of Asiatic Studies*, Vol. 49 [2], 1989): pp. 429-430.

p. 401, 'Croesus, Lord of Lydia'
Line 2: *Sicherheit*, a German word which effortlessly combines the senses of several English ones, including 'security, safety, surety', as well as 'certainty, efficiency, safeguard, confidence, assurance'.

p. 404, 'What the Delphic Oracle said'
For Anne Stevenson.

p. 406, 'The foiler fooled'
Line 15: *Atishoo all fall down*: chorus line of the English nursery rhyme 'Ring a ring o' roses', popularly believed to describe the effects of the Great Plague of London, 1665-1666.

p. 408, '*Thunder rolling*'
Lines 15-17: see *Hamlet*, Act III, Sc. 1, lines 85-86.

p. 409, 'Let her'
The names are of sky-gods and storm-gods in various mythologies.

p. 414, 'In the storm's eye'
In memory of Ted Hughes (1930–1998).

pp.415-422, 'STILLING'
For Shi Jing.

p. 416, '*He left his city*'
For Zhang Shaozhou.

p. 419, 'Approximations'
Wu wei in line 2 is repeated in the base-line, 无为: lit. 'without doing' or 'without acting, being, becoming' See the note on p. 553 to 'Before you go', p. 330, and also 'Nothing happens', p. 421, and 'Ringing his bowl-bell', p. 422.

p. 420, 'The ringing, *zhong*, the centre'
For 中 (*zhong*) in the base-line, see the note on p. 538 above to 'Judge and jury', p. 48.

p. 421, 'Nothing happens'.

For 无为 (*wu wei*) in the base-line, see the notes on p. 553 to 'Before you go', p. 330, and on p. 557 to 'Approximations', p. 419, and the next note.

p. 422, 'Ringing his bowl-bell'

Lines 12-13: compare "Those who hear the sound of a sound are deaf. Those who hear the sound of no sound are discerning. Those who are neither deaf nor discerning have penetrated through to spirit illumination." Liu An, King of Huainan, *The Huainanzi*, 2010 [139 BCE], ch. 17, section 18, (New York, NY: Columbia University Press): p. 669. For 无为 (*wu wei*) in the base-line, see: the notes on p. 553 to 'Before you go', p. 330; and on p. 557 to 'Approximations, p. 419; and above to 'Nothing happens', p. 421.

p. 424, '*Mountain fir*'

For Nasos Vayenas. Based on a passage in the *Iliad*, Book 14:

ἔνθ' Ὕπνος μὲν ἔμεινε πάρος Διὸς ὄσσε ἰδέσθαι
εἰς ἐλάτην ἀναβὰς περιμήκετον, ἣ τότ' ἐν Ἴδῃ
μακροτάτη πεφυυῖα δι' ἠέρος αἰθέρ' ἵκανεν

Sleep then stopped, before Zeus' eyes could see him,
climbed a high pine tree, at that time the tallest one
growing on Ida. It stretched up through the lower air ('aer')
right into the sky ('aether').

(Tr. Ian Johnston, online at https://records.viu.ca/~/school archive/ Classes/fulltext/www.mala.bc.ca/~johnstoi/homer/iliad_title.htm. Reconsulted, July 27, 2016). The point of interest here is the distinction between 'air' and 'aether', and how these terms are to be understood today. See Charles H. Kahn, *Anaximander and the Origins of Greek Cosmology*, 1994, (Indianapolis, IN: Hackett): pp. 133–145, esp. p. 145.

p. 425, 'Wild geese'

For Edward L. Shaughnessy. For his commentary on the imagem of geese in hexagram 53, see his *Before Confucius: Studies in the Creation of the Chinese* Classics, 1997 (Albany, NY: State University of New York Press): pp. 21-23. See also his *I Ching, the Classic of Change: the first English translation of the newly discovered second-century B. C. Mawangdui texts*, 1996 (New York, NY: Ballantine Books): pp. 11-12.

p. 426, 'River-run'
For Vera V. Radojević. See also the companion poem, 'River-run, river-ruin', p. 476.

p. 427, 'A challenge'
For Lee Moden.

p. 429, 'What the tinker said (2)'
For Gully Burns and Cat Buranahirun. See also the companion piece, 'What the tinker said (1)', p. 82.

p. 432, '*Push me, said the girl*'
Lines 10-11 come from 'The Fair Flower of Northumberland', ballad no. 9, *The English and Scottish Popular Ballads*, ed. Francis James Child, vol. 1, 1965 (New York, NY: Dover Publications): pp. 111–118.

p. 435, '*Hoy le ha entrado una astilla*'
From a poem by César Vallejo. See his *Complete Later Poems 1923–1938*, eds. & trs. Valentino Gianuzzi and Michael Smith, 2005 (Exeter: Shearsman Books): pp. 230-23. See also '*C'est la vie, mort de la Mort!*', p. 333 and '*El libro de la naturaleza*', p. 338.

pp. 439-446, 'ABOUNDING, BRIMMING'
For Michael and Mary Rowan-Robinson.

p. 440, '*Things, brimming*'
To honour George Oppen (1908–1994) and for Michael Heller.

p. 441, 'Adhering, inhering'
For Katica Kulavkova.

p. 443. 'Consoling, Abundant, Terrifying Stars'
See also 'Heaven-stuff', p.445.

p. 444, 'What Zhang Zai said'
For Catherine Ng. See also: 'What Zhang Zai thought', p. 6, and the note on p. 535; and also 'What Zhang Zai knew', p. 446, and the note to it on p. 560. For lines 1-2, see Ira E. Kasoff, *The Thought of Chang Tsai,* 1984 (Cambridge: Cambridge University Press): p. 56.

p. 445, 'Heaven-stuff'
The opening lines echo Blaise Pascal's dictum, "Le silence éternel de ces espaces infinis m'effraie," *Pensées*, iii. 206. This echo is linked with Caliban's speech in *The Tempest,* Act III, Sc. 2, lines 129-130: "Be not

afeard. The isle is full of noises, / Sounds, and sweet airs that give delight and hurt not." See also 'Consoling, Abundant, Terrifying Stars', p. 443.

p. 446, ' What Zhang Zai knew'
See the companion pieces: 'What Zhang Zai thought', p. 6, and the note on p. 535; and 'What Zhang Zai said', p. 444, and the note on p. 559. See also Ira E. Kasoff, *The Thought of Chang Tsai*, 1984 (Cambridge: Cambridge University Press): pp. 53-65.

pp. 447-454, 'Travelling'
For philip kuhn.

p. 452, 'Now I confess'
For Anthony Rudolf. For 道 (*dao*) in the base-line, see the note on p. 541 to 'Way', p. 120.

p. 457, 'Father, counting'
See also the two companion pieces, 'Child, counting', p. 32, and 'Child, calculating', p. 37, and the notes on. pp. 537.

p. 460, 'Wild creatures'
In memory of Peter Mansfield (1942–2009), and a response to his unpublished poem 'Credo', written between 1961 and 1964, when he was an undergraduate at Pembroke College, Cambridge:

> It is not our business
> we who have set out
> to ask formulable questions
> but in our passing to distil
> answers from the lies of circumstance.
>
> In the forest we must hear
> behind the noise the young whisper
> and scent not only this roebuck but him
> in the next valley or the afternext
> dissatisfied:
>
> our bodies a nostril and a leap
> our minds the only formless question
> and acquiescence, in the ritual
> of expectancy not hope
> We are not liars. We are not priests.

This poem by my student contemporary and friend has had a pervasive influence on my thinking for over 50 years.

p. 464, '*Two lakes, joined*'
In memory of Frances Richards (1903–1985). The Derwent and the Ladybower are artificial lakes in the Peak District, Derbyshire, England. This poem was the first in *Changing* to be written directly out of a consultation of the *I Ching*, August 30, 1984: see the 'POSTSCRIPT', p. 524 above. A separate essay on the composition of this poem is forthcoming. See also p. 334, 'The complete art of drowning'.

pp. 465 and 466, 'Lakeside' and 'Past Coppice Island'
For John Matthias.

p. 470, 'Hail Victory'
The title translates the Nazi chant, '*Sieg Heil.*' Base-line: *these were the 'Wing'd-with-Awe'* … *Inviolable*: from Ezra Pound's poem 'The Return', *Selected Poems*, 1971 [1928] (London: Faber and Faber): p. 85.

p. 474, 'Escaping'
For Dan Burt.

p. 476, 'River-run, river-ruin'
In memory of Peter Russell (1921–2003). See also the companion-poem, 'River-run', p. 426.

pp. 477 and 478, 'For Natalie, dying' and 'Rowan tree, the day after her departure'
For Natalie Rein, née Blisson (1932–2001).

p. 480, '*Economies*'
For Lara Burns.

p. 488, '*Ring of truth*'
For Daša Marić.

p. 489, 'Inanna's Descent'
For Hilary Davies.

p. 490, 'Seagull's wings'
For Daša Marić.

p. 491, 'At Shipwreck Head'
Homage to Wang Liping. See also the companion poem, 'At Dragon Gate', p. 158, and the note on p. 543.

pp. 493 and 494, 'Ghost revisiting' and 'Ghost, questioning'
In memory of Alexander Berengarten, *aka* Burns (1901–1947). Both poems are based on a dream.

p. 498, 'Timbre of her voice'
In memory of Rosalind Burns, née Taylor (1911–1968).

p. 499, 'Looking for [the] Revolution'
In memory of Iulian K. Shchutskii (1897–1938). See his *Researches on the I Ching*, tr. William L. MacDonald and Tsuyoshi Hasegawa with Hellmut Wilhelm, 1980 [1937], esp. the 'Biographical Sketch' by N. A. Petrov (London: Routledge and Kegan Paul): pp. lxv-lxvi. See also Khayutina, Maria *et al.*, 'Sinological Profiles, Iulian Shchutskii', online at http://www.umass.edu/wsp/sinology/persons/shchutskii.htm. Reconsulted, August 5, 2015.

p. 504, '*Odyssified*'
In memory of Kimon Friar (1911–1993), translator of Nikos Kazantzakis' *The Odyssey: a Modern Sequel*, 1958 (New York, NY: Simon and Schuster).

p. 506, 'In faint distress'
For John Matthias.

p. 507, 'Merlin to young Arthur'
See also the companion pieces, '*Young Arthur*', p. 152, and 'The end of Arthur', p. 157.

p. 508, 'Necessary repairs'
For Paul Pines.

p. 510, 'First bricks'
For Douglas and Marjorie Kinsey.

p. 514, 'In rat light'
For Thomas Cleary.

p. 515, 'Eyes open forward'
In memory of Peter Mansfield (1942–2009). See also the note on pp. 560-1 to 'Wild creatures'.

p. 516, 'Ready steady go'
For Anthony Rudolf.

p. 517, 'Alchymical perle'

For Carl Schmidt. The first lines are adapted from the English medieval poem *Pearl* (*Perle*), ed. E. V. Gordon, 1953 [1958] (Oxford: Clarendon Press): pp. 2-3.

p. 518, 'Brightness, diffusing'

For Paschalis Nikolaou. With regard to 易 (*yi*) in the base-line, long after writing this poem I discovered that one of the explanations proposed for the origin of the graph, which occurs in the title of the *Book of Changes* (易經), is an earlier pair of graphs meaning 'increase'. In the first chapter of his Ph.D. thesis, Bent Nielsen cites several 20th century Chinese scholars who argue that the graph's two "archaic forms" are "abridged forms of a more complex pictograph showing a pair of hands holding an ewer and pouring something, probably wine, into a goblet." See 'The Meaning of *Yi* 易', in *The Qian Zuo Du* 乾鑿度: *A Late Han Dynasty (202 B.C. – A.D. 220) Study of the Book of Changes, Yi jing* 易經, 1995 (University of Copenhagen: Faculty of Humanities): p. 32. See also the note to the FRONT COVER on p. 533 above; and 'The force that fills and empties', p. 20. Lines 14-15 echo Ezra Pound: see 'A yellow lower garment', p. 19, and the note on p. 536.

CPSIA information can be obtained
at www.ICGtesting.com
Printed in the USA
LVHW101105141122
733086LV00005B/188